CU01464056

To Granny and Grandad
Love from Sean
13/11/99

Celebration 2000

CATCH THE MILLENNIUM BUG WITH ISRIG AND

YOUNG WRITERS

LEICESTERSHIRE

Edited by Allison Dowse

First published in Great Britain in 1999 by
YOUNG WRITERS
Remus House,
Coltsfoot Drive,
Woodston,
Peterborough, PE2 9JX
Telephone (01733) 890066

All Rights Reserved

Copyright Contributors 1999

HB ISBN 0 75431 614 9
SB ISBN 0 75431 615 7

FOREWORD

Young Writers have produced poetry books in conjunction with schools for over eight years; providing a platform for talented young people to shine. This year, the Celebration 2000 collection of regional anthologies were developed with the millennium in mind.

With the nation taking stock of how far we have come, and reflecting on what we want to achieve in the future, our anthologies give a vivid insight into the thoughts and experiences of the younger generation.

We were once again impressed with the quality and attention to detail of every entry received and hope you will enjoy the poems we have decided to feature in *Celebration 2000 Leicestershire* for many years to come.

CONTENTS

Burbage Junior School

Zoé Funnell	15
Dale Peppitt	16
Charlotte Burns	16
Imogen Jones	17
Nicola Griffiths	17
Craig Norman	18
Robyn Brandrick	18
Emily Dickinson	19
Ryan Holdback	19
Chloe Charles	20
Scott Brown	20
Nikki Cooper	21
Rebecca Rose	22
Natalie Kent	22
Sarah Dolphin	23
Thomas Edwards	24
Charlotte Davis	25
Paul Marriot	25
Ashley Warren	26
Emma Warrington	26
Lara Lewis	27
Kate Healey	28
Liam Palmer	28
Max Stephenson	29
Alex Botting	30

Church Langton Primary School

Jodie Watts	30
Suzanne Ward	31
Annie Bladon	31
Nicholas Ruggles	31
Kayleigh Hibbert	32
Kieran Soni	32
Philip Durno	32
Gavin Hudspith	33
Matthew Watson	33
Tom Lambert	33

Emily Slatter	34
Cally Holland	34
Nicholas Hollis & Harry Lewis	35
Alicia Higham	35
Katie Muggleton	36
Ayesha Emilie Edwards	36
Emma Ruggles	37
Craig Freestone	37
Debora Tugwell	38
Lucie Hartley	39
Rochelle Lambert	39
Hayley Giles	40
Nicola Jayne Robinson	40
Sally Weston	40
Louise Smerdon	41
Lucy Parkin	41

Fleckney Primary School

Georgina Cullen	42
Kimberley Leiser	42
Naomi Clough	43
Joshua Buck	43
Louis Swann	44
Hamish Graham	44
Matthew Dakin	45
Nichola Ellison	45
Zoe Townsend	46
Sam McKenna	46
Kelly McClymont	47
Emma Faulkner	47
Joe Riley	48
Rachael Handley	48
Oliver Crompton	49
Abby Lockwood-Jones	49
Mark Redfearn	50
Daniel Gluyas	50
Hannah Crabtree	51
Eleanor Moss	51

Samantha Fell	70
Emma Haig	71
Christian Moroney	72

Normanton-On-Soar Primary School

Jasper Heaton	73
Rachael Ward	74
Hayley Wilson	74
Emma Allard	74
Amy Waldron	75
Victoria Hellier	75

Old Mill Primary School

Jack Constant	76
Christopher French	76
Sophie Hayward	77
Jennifer Sullivan	77
Lisa Preston	78
Natasha McLean Pender	78
Jasmine Cockerill	79
Edward Winnington	79
Rebecca Godden	80
Anna Larkins	80
Ruth Bott	81
Charlotte Smith	81
Nicole Arnold	82
Hannah Burton	82
Sarah Ward	82
Sam Reynolds	83
Jordan Spencer	83
Sarah McSharry	84
Sam Estill	84
Hannah Symington	85
Rebecca Tongue	85
Ryan Kenyon	86
Hannah Kedie	86
Wayne Harris	87
Ashley Voss	87

Christopher Hinton	88
David James Mingay	88
Nicola Knott	89
Philip Chambers	89
Lucy Mulvany	90
Darren Latkowski	90
Clare Alison Wright	90

Orchard CP School, Castle Donington

Oliver Stephenson	91
Millie Maddocks	91
David Gerrard	92
Daniel Abbey	92
Christopher Marshall	93
Kelly Rayns	94
Michael Byrne	95
Sarra Elliott	95
Craig Saddington	96
Anthony Watts	96
Megan Palframan	97
Hannah Clifton	98
Leanne Gale	99
Laura Faley	100
Marc Ryan	101
Hayley Sly	102
Sarah Stallard	102
Rebecca Houghton	103
Hayley Warren	103
Helen MacIver	104

Orchard Primary School, Broughton Astley

Stephen Oliff	104
Charlotte Joanne Kenney	104
Jessie Laura Morris	105
Luke Murgatroyd	106
Donald Robertson	106
Sam Williams	107
Roxanne Herbert	107

The Poems

TOXIC WASTE

Don't throw litter,
don't throw waste,
you should see the poor fish's face.

Poor little fish swimming around,
not any more he's on the shelly ground.

Oil tank spills,
the sea it fills
by the second.
The poor little fish,
he is threatened.

Eddie Hamilton (10)
Brooke Hill Primary School

POLLUTION

I love the deep blue sea,
it's a special place to be.
Keep it safe and true
for me and you.
Keep the beach nice and clean
so the fish can be seen.
Pollution is very bad
and it would make me sad,
if there were no fish in the
deep blue sea.

Sean Doyle (10)
Brooke Hill Primary School

POLLUTION

The ship spills its oil,
the birds they do toil,
we battle all weathers
to clean the birds' feathers.
The fish where they land
lay dead on the sand,
the sea is still thick
with remains of the slick.
In time it will clear,
too late, I do fear
for the creatures of the sea
who depend on you and me.
Will continue to pay the price
unless we keep the world nice.

Laura Sleightholme (9)
Brooke Hill Primary School

LIFE AND DEATH

When I go to sleep,
I think about where I come from
I wish I knew who I was before,
I really wish I knew God and the after-life,
why heaven and why hell, what for?
In some dreams I imagine the after-life
I see my dog Lassie in dreams.
I really want to see you again Lassie,
where are you please Lassie?
Please tell me where are you?
When I die, I hope I see you again.

Marcus Hudson (9)
Brooke Hill Primary School

POLLUTION

All those jars, cans and tins
are meant to go in the bins.
All of this is pollution,
there has to be a solution.
Don't use your car,
walk if it's not far.
It's a good idea
to keep Britain clear
by picking up litter,
it will keep you much fitter.
The oil slick all slimy and thick
makes the creatures sick.
If we don't all try,
then the Earth will die.

Luke Arnold (9)
Brooke Hill Primary School

THE EARTH

People are dropping lots of litter,
it's making lots of people titter.
If we could only stop this lark,
the world would be clean, without a mark.
It would be horrible if we were left
to pollute the Earth,
this is the only chance we get.
People are dropping lots of litter,
it's making lots of people titter.
They're laughing because they don't care.

Roz Glynn (10)
Brooke Hill Primary School

WHEN

When the seagulls fly in the air,
when the fish swim in the sea,
when nature is at its peak of beauty.

When man comes,
when man comes with oil,
when man comes with sewage,
when man comes with toxic fumes.

That's when the seagulls no longer fly,
that's when the fish no longer swim,
that's when nature is disregarded,
that's when nature is disrespected,
that's when nature's beauty is gone.
All it's beauty gone,
destroyed by man.

That's when man tries to clean up,
that's when the damage is done.

Perinne Kirby (10)
Brooke Hill Primary School

MY TWO VERY BEST FRIENDS

I have got two best friends,
they are Catherine and Lauren.
I met Lauren first, but Catherine is still one of my best.
Catherine lends me things and keeps me company.
Lauren's got to be there when I need a friend.
Lauren's got this habit of smelling things,
Catherine wiggles her nose.
I'd be lost without them.

Harriet Leefe (9)
Brooke Hill Primary School

I WONDER?

I wonder what could be the solution
for all of the world's dreadful pollution.
All the waste gases released
into the air,
are making up acid rain
and it's not fair.
The birds and the bees will
have no place to go,
because the forest and trees
are dying,
didn't you know?
We must all look after the world
because it's up to you and me
to make it a healthy
and happy place to be.

Charlotte Powell (9)
Brooke Hill Primary School

MICO

My best friend is Mico,
he is as soft as a fluffy toy.
He is like a leopard, but white
with orange spots,
and something I find strange is that he
circles the garden.
Together we have climbed huge hills
and even moved house together.
His paws always get muddy, I don't mind.
but my mum does!
My best friend is my dog.

Ryan Thwaites (10)
Brooke Hill Primary School

SORRY

I've never, ever felt so sad,
please forgive me,
I feel so bad.

I'll write it in a letter,
I'll phone you up,
I'm sure things will be better.

I wish I hadn't done such a thing,
I wish I had stopped and thought,
who knows what this will bring?

I know I shouldn't ask,
I am being very rude,
please forgive me fast.

Can't we make it up,
I'm so sad.
It would be like winning the world cup,
I'm very, very, very, very, very, very, sorry.

Catherine Allen (10)
Brooke Hill Primary School

GOD

The sunrise in the morning,
the golden sand in the afternoon,
the cold snow in the winter,
the sparkling stars in the night,
the different coloured blossom
on the trees in April,
they make me think about God.

Katie Hibbitt (9)
Brooke Hill Primary School

SONG OF A DEER

I am a gentle animal
as I prance around the forest
elegantly,
but I am an easy prey.

My coat is smooth like leather,
I am a quiet animal,
but I am an easy prey.

I feed only on grass
and make a noise unknown to man,
but I am an easy prey.

Emma Brown (9)
Brooke Hill Primary School

MYSELF!

I love my leaping, lanky legs,
and my enchanting, eager eyes,
my white and sparkly toothy pegs
and my mouth that sometimes lies.
I love my golden, gleaming hair,
and my brain, well
it's rather insane!
And my speech, I really do share,
and occasionally, I sometimes
do swear!
But really I think I am
a real big pain!

Emma Pietrzak (11)
Brookside Primary School

DARKNESS

Darkness creeps, darkness crawls,
over the ceiling, up the walls.

Through cracks and crevices,
under the door,
it does not stop,
as it floats on the floor.

Every room in the house,
it goes into, quiet as a mouse.

Over obstacles, under too,
when it hits more darkness, it grows and grows.

As daylight comes
the clock strikes six,
the darkness vanishes
like burning sticks.

Darkness doesn't creep, darkness doesn't crawl,
disappears by the ceiling,
seeps into the wall.

Nicholas Mortimer (11)
Brookside Primary School

THE LAZY KID

You sat there staring at the window,
with nothing but looking to do.
The teacher was shouting her head off,
with everybody staring at you.

Mathew Smeeton (10)
Brookside Primary School

I USED TO

I used to missspell,
ignore capitals,
Miss out punctuation
Join wordstogether when I shouldn't,
But worst of all, I used to always forget to finish
what I was . . .

Emma Booth (11)
Brookside Primary School

A HAPPY GARDEN DAY

The dusty path leads its way
on the lush, luscious grass that springs
and the stream merrily gurgles.
The apple trees sticking out of the blue sky,
what a lovely experience.

Adam Summers (9)
Brookside Primary School

MY FAMILY

I have a sister, she is a pest.
I love my mum, she is the best.
My brother, he plays football for a club,
my mum and my dad like to go to the pub.

Tom Stewart (10)
Brookside Primary School

BALLAD OF A STRANDED CLASS

It happened in September of 1993,
a class of children and their teacher went for a trip to the sea.
They explored the cave and found a punctured, smelly ball,
they forgot about the time and night began to fall.
The waves were zooming inwards up the cold sand,
the wind was splashing round cliffs and the seaspray splashing land,
the rain came down and soaked them and the sharp cliffs leant in,
and the mist was falling quickly, like a thick, strong metal bin.

The teacher was shouting to the children in the fog,
the wind blew round pale faces and the waves brought up a log.
the girls started screaming, the boys began to shout,
the cliffs were leaning inwards as they shouted 'Let us out.'
But the old fisherman heard them
from his grimy, gloomy tower,
and all were safe and well again
in less than half an hour.

Ailsa Pierson (9)
Brookside Primary School

THE WOOD

I see a bat come swooping down,
a witch on a broom flying past the full moon.
Trees look like hands.
The sky is all gloomy.
Grass up to your knees.
The moon is all spooky.
Twigs are snapping on the ground,
and owl is hooting in a tree.
There's no one here except you and me.

Jessica Duma (9)
Brookside Primary School

Snow

Smooth snow, like icing on a cake,
making it into snowballs,
throwing them on the lake.
Ice on the pond's all frozen solid.
Children sledge down the hill
into the ditch at the bottom.
But not me, I'm staying inside,
where it's warm and cosy.

Rachel Simpson (9)
Brookside Primary School

Stars

Glittering stars in the
shining, dark sky
when the sun slowly fades
into a moon.

Katie Shahatit (9)
Brookside Primary School

Trust

Trust is my worthy toys,
trust is a snappy crocodile,
trust is my adventurous mum,
trust is my sparkly, white dwarf book,
trust is my cosy bed,
trust is my black, shiny jeans,
trust is a creamy, yellow banana,
trust is my trustful home.

Ben Pakenham-Walsh (10)
Brookside Primary School

SIMILE POEM

The writer of this poem is . . .
as athletic as Tim Henman,
as football mad as Ronaldo,
as daring as a lion feeder,
as ugly as an
elephant's backside!
The writer of this poem
never ceases to amaze.
She's one in a million, billion
(or so this poem says.)

Natalie Way (10)
Brookside Primary School

A SIMILE POEM

The writer of this poem is . . .
as greedy as a pig,
as quiet as a mouse,
as happy as the sun,
as dramatic as Mr Bean.
The writer of this poem
never ceases to amaze,
he's one in a million, billion,
or so this poem says.

Stephen Westwood (9)
Brookside Primary School

THE MAN AND HIS BOOK!

The grass was as green as a cucumber,
his hat had a bright red brim.
A hundred and seven was his page number,
and his book was 'Swan in the Swim.'

His parasol kept him shaded,
from the springtime sun.
The trees were green and had faded,
and he found reading was oh so much fun.

Becci Powell (10)
Brookside Primary School

THE WOODS

Twigs crunching
sticky mud,
short trees,
long grass
all in one dark night!
Stars glowing,
owls hooting,
trees rustling,
leaves falling,
it gave me a fright!

Sarah Brown (10)
Brookside Primary School

WINTER

People all wrapped up and children on their sledges
and I can hear a robin singing in the hedges.
People throwing snowballs and jumping in the snow
and I can see people's fingers glow.
People are ice skating, they're slipping and they're sliding
and even children are playing, laughing and hiding.
As I go down on my sledge, I say *weeee*
and nearly run into a tree.
I fell off with my dad, we went very fast,
but at last, *crash, smash* my sledge broke.
I'm cold, I want to go home.
My voice is so croaky, and I'm freezing. Goodbye.

Chloe Bishop (10)
Brookside Primary School

SIMILE POEM

The writer of this poem
is as cute as a ginger cat,
like a footballing maniac,
as hairy as two chimpanzees,
as mad as a wasp just about to sting.
The writer of this poem
never ceases to amaze,
he's one in a million,
or so the poem says.

Grant Newcombe (9)
Brookside Primary School

CHRISTMAS

Christmas is a jolly time, a happy time, a holly time.
Santa leaves presents under the tree,
presents that will later fill us with glee.
We have turkey, carrots and stuffing,
a meal that will leave us huffing and puffing.
Making snowmen, going sledging,
at the bottom into hedging!

Peter Gwynne (9)
Brookside Primary School

THE WIND

The wind is a hysterical man.
At night, he rages, raves and fires.
This glum man kicks the pebbles on the drive,
he grumbles, moans and mumbles,
you can hear him cry at night.
He whines, whimpers, croons and rumbles.
He snaps and snarls at the babies
crying in their cots.
He swishes his tail to and fro,
swish, swash, swish, swash
until dawn comes.
He kicks the frosted leaves and
dances to the tune of the grass.
he pushes the babies' cradles
and sings a lullaby.
He blows the children's chubby faces
to keep them cool,
blow, blow, blow, blow!

Zoé Funnell (10)
Burbage Junior School

THE WIND

The wind is like a wild man,
he swirls and whirls, drying washing on every line.
He whistles to make the grass sway,
he flicks up leaves off every lawn, with his brittle fingers.

He blows furiously with his raging breath,
he kicks every car or object in sight with his ferocious feet.
He picks up buildings with his indestructible hands.

He kicks and blows, he pushes, he pulls,
he blows every flower, he shakes every bush,
he hears every child kick each tiny leaf, with his keen ears.
But at night, you can hear his soft snoring as he peacefully sleeps.

Dale Peppitt (11)
Burbage Junior School

LAST DAYS OF SUMMER

The sun was shining, the birds were singing,
and the grass is glowing in the sunlight.
At night the stars were startling, like
strikes of sandy starlight.
Summer is a time when people swim in the pool,
they sunbathe in the glittering sun.
Children ride on bikes up and down the street.
The cold weather came,
everyone went indoors to watch the rain
pour down. It's made large puddles
on the paths, the roads, the streets.
We leave our wellies outside to dry.
Summer's gone, and what's gone is gone.

Charlotte Burns (10)
Burbage Junior School

THE LAST DAYS OF SUMMER

The flowers are bending over backwards,
like branches on an old willow tree.
The night is creeping in like a tiger
getting ready for action.
The dew drops on spiders webs
like tiny diamonds glimmering in the light.
The shadows are getting longer,
like a giant walking in front of you.
The daytime isn't as it was,
like the sun is disintegrating, bit by bit.
The shorts and tee shirts are packed away
like all your old toys.
There is a bitter wind, like
it's stretching out to bite you.
The clouds are covering, like a
big, black cloth.
The rain splashes down, making little rivers.

Imogen Jones (9)
Burbage Junior School

THE LAST DAYS OF SUMMER

The dew on the cobwebs gleams at me as if they are made of silver.
The clouds are getting darker, as if winter wants to come early.
The shadows are larger as if the trees are growing every second.
The mornings are darker as if night was still there.
The flowers are dying back like one touch would make them
shrivel up and die.
The rain is colder now, like ice falling from the sky.

Nicola Griffiths (9)
Burbage Junior School

LAST DAYS OF SUMMER

The clouds are like candy-floss that's been
dipped in a dark blue sauce.

The shadows are longer, like black giants
coming to have a fight.

The flowers are like an old grandma's
shrivelled skin.

The cool wind is blowing the trees,
like they are shaking their whole bodies around.

The cool air is like brushing your teeth
with a minty toothpaste.

Craig Norman (10)
Burbage Junior School

THE LAST DAYS OF SUMMER

It's cold, it's windy and the dew is
on the grass, shining brightly.
The flowers are shrivelling into
little brown balls which crack
when you drop them on the floor.
The sun is disappearing into the
grey sky.
The air is cool, like a spearmint Polo.
The grey clouds are like a big, grey
balloon of smoke and rain.
The leaves are just starting to drop off
massive oak trees.

Robyn Brandrick (9)
Burbage Junior School

THE LAST DAYS OF SUMMER

The last days of summer are disappearing,
and shadows are getting longer by the day.
Flowers are fading away, like a hedgehog
curled up ready for the winter.
Nobody wants to go out in shorts and tee shirts
anymore.
The wind is getting fiercer, like a lion who wants his lunch.
The clouds are getting darker, like puffs of black smoke.
Every night it gets blacker than the night before.
Birds are abandoning the country fast, to get away from
the freezing winter which will come after the on-coming
autumn.
The dew is like crystals that glimmer in the morning
sunlight.
Sometimes, it's chilly and frosty, but not most of the time.

Emily Dickinson (9)
Burbage Junior School

LAST DAYS OF SUMMER

The last few days of summer,
the birds began to sing,
the plants began to fall and die
in the soft, brown soil.
As the days become shorter,
the years seem longer,
the nights get darker.

I still remember my holiday,
when I went to Spain in an aeroplane.
The seas were cold and sands were golden.
The last days of summer are over.

Ryan Holdback (9)
Burbage Junior School

LAST DAYS OF SUMMER

Summer days are nearly done!
All the fun and enjoyment won.
Swinging high, swinging low,
round and round on the merry-go.

But now autumn leaves
blow, blow, blow,
not to grow, no! Oh no!
To fall low, to carpet the ground
now the rain is falling,
splish, splash, splosh!
Now the wind is howling,
howl, howl, howl!

Autumn here, autumn gone!
Winter's coldness has begun.
Snow is sparkling as it falls,
snowballs thrown,
snowman made with his little carrot nose!

Summer seems so far away,
that I had the fun and heat to play!

Chloe Charles (10)
Burbage Junior School

THE WIND

The wind is a wild man,
he kicks with his ferocious feet,
and pulls the swaying trees with his mighty fingers.
Blowing roofs off houses,
he is the king of destruction.

Or on the other hand,
he can be as gentle as a baby,
and as calm as the sea on a pleasant summer morning.
He pushes the small waves coming up the shore,
moving the stones up and down,
whistling as he scuttles along the beach.

Scott Brown (10)
Burbage Junior School

THE WIND

The wind is a ferocious man,
howling in the trees.
Every path he takes, he is destroying
everything in sight.
His eyes as sharp as an eagle's,
he sees us as devils from hell.
He has horns like a bull, butting the trees,
and knocks them down as well.

The calm wind however, is a kind woman,
rustling the plants.
She whistles to make the birds sing, so God can rest.
She sees us as angels, beautiful and good.
She has no horns, but only hair.
She only wishes to be fair.

Mostly, they fight in rage,
arguing over who will blow.
Finally they decide.
The one that lost the fight rests on a cloud
and waits for their turn.

Nikki Cooper (10)
Burbage Junior School

THE GREAT GREY WIND

The wind is an old, grey man.
He whispers past your ear on a pleasant summer's day.
He rocks the trees gently
and pushes the clouds high in the sky.

Then he roars, he roars with almighty force,
his hoary hair trailing behind him.
He runs, he runs, he runs,
he crashes into cliffs,
he bashes into trees,
he pushes past houses.

The evening draws on,
he soon grows very weary.
He lies gently on the floor
and listens to the silence all around him.
No noise, no noise, nothing.

Rebecca Rose (10)
Burbage Junior School

THE WIND

The wind is a widowed woman.
She picks at the paralysed petals with her fragile fingers,
and wades through the tender grass.
She runs around the tree tops as her tattered hair
drags behind, whipping her face.

Sometimes she cries a tearful song
as the moon glows in the night sky.
Sometimes she bangs on the cracking windows
trying to waste her anger.

A kite flies high in the sky whilst she whistles
in and out.
Silence as it falls to the ground with barely
any sound.

When it starts to rain,
she always happens to complain.
Twirling, curling up the leaves that glide through
the air,
until the dawn starts to appear.

Natalie Kent (11)
Burbage Junior School

THE WIND

The wind is a wild woman,
each day in a different mood.
Some days she would cry out
and stamp with her transparent feet.
If you dare tease her
she will lash out and strike you down.
At night, she's still there,
tearing, throwing, like a restless puppy.
Continuing through the night,
she rips up turf and soil
in an angry mood.
With skimming eyes, she looks around,
she sees someone being bullied
and so opens her tender mouth
and blows the bully away,
then pulls her lips together,
ready to brew more wind.
She is pleased.

Sarah Dolphin (10)
Burbage Junior School

THE WINDY MOODS

The wind is a temperamental man,
evil and terrifying.
Flying like a bird through the secluded village,
blowing at trees like a half-hearted dragon, ripping the land,
making them bow down to him as the birds fly away in alarm
from the savage, temperamental man.
The menacing man, pulling petals off plants innocently,
in a childish way,
he blows with his capable lungs at defenceless grass and shouts
in anger if he does not succeed.
He is furious and ferocious, fuming and incensed, raging and boiling,
biting and raving, and very evil.

The wind is a helpful woman,
calm and friendly,
skipping and hopping through the peaceful village,
blowing at meadow hay and scarecrow hats,
brushing gently through the fur of cats,
kicking and waving at washing, helpfully blowing it dry.
She gives the plants and trees a warm, stroking breeze.

In the desert, the wind is an old-aged man,
glum and beaten by the sun,
scorched and torched,
and viciously stares at the arid sunshine.
He wanders around the vast, sandy distance,
and as the glum, old, withered man, not strong and forceful,
lays down to rest,
scorched and burned, fired up and badly hurt, parched and
frazzled, tedious and awfully shrivelled, blistered and roasted,
baked and sweltered, he goes on giving out a weak breeze.

Thomas Edwards (11)
Burbage Junior School

THE OBSTREPEROUS WIND

The wind is a wild woman,
rocking weak fences from side to side,
thrashing down trees with her ferocious fingers.
She blows dainty petals off flowers,
scattering them over the swaying grass,
exasperation on her face.

Soon she calms down,
her temper disappearing.
A performing ballet dancer
twirling through trees,
breathing deeply for her whistling competition,
which she hopes she will win.

Mischievously, she takes a hat or two,
a stealthy robber,
tiptoeing through the undergrowth,
hiding behind bushes,
waiting for her grand finale.

Charlotte Davis (11)
Burbage Junior School

LITTER!

Worms sliding over old cans,
like slime from a baby after his dinner.
An old rusty car,
beetles pouring from it,
like a black swamp,
litter blowing in the wind,
like a powerful tornado.

Paul Marriot (9)
Burbage Junior School

THE WIND IS A WILD WOMAN

The wind is a wild woman.
She kicks up leaves with her ferocious feet,
she shakes down leaves with her fragile fingers,
she bad-temperedly pulls up the colourful kite
and pulls the man across the field.

She calmly whistles through the uncut grass.
She sprints through trees, bounces off branches,
she leaps over fences, garden to garden
as if practising the 100 metre hurdles.

She removes harmless flowers and throws them away,
she kicks down fences with her high-heeled boots
then destroys them with no bother.
She is in a foul-tempered mood.
The wind is a wild woman.

Ashley Warren (10)
Burbage Junior School

THE SAVAGE WIND

The wind is a wild woman,
doing just as she pleases.
In an angry mood, she whirls around
hitting everything in her path.

Then she stops and carefully turns around,
not knowing what to do next.
She pleasantly skips around the trees,
whistling like a summer breeze.

She walks along the stony path,
scuffing her feet on the floor,
picking up litter, then scattering it about,
so tired, so dreary, so sleepy.

Then once again, she tiptoes home
to give the world a rest.
She settles upon the fluffy clouds
and whistles the world to sleep.

Emma Warrington (11)
Burbage Junior School

THE TORMENTING WIND

The wind is a brutal woman,
she shifts up leaves with her clasping hands.
She cracks open nuts with the power she possesses.
Swoosh! She opens gates and tortures
small fragile flowers.

She can see the whole world,
and can smell the delicious and ghastly smells,
she feels the birds and touches the people,
and she hears herself rushing
and birds huddled together, twittering.

Now she is calm,
she rests on the tops of trees,
and swiftly floats around.
She doesn't push or pull, but
she walks so quietly,
that no one can hear.

Lara Lewis (10)
Burbage Junior School

THE WIND

The wind is a whistling woman,
she walks through the crunchy leaves,
kicking them into the air with her fragile feet.
As she kicks, her temper worsens
and her breath sighs heavily.

Soon she calms.
As she sweeps her dress through her garden gate,
she pegs her washing out and rocks the line to dry.

Then she picks at the elegant petals and
blows them into the night sky.
Being naughty, she takes a hat or two,
then twirls it off into space,
where it is lost forever.

Kate Healey (11)
Burbage Junior School

THE WICKED, WILD, WIND

The wicked, wild wind is a ferocious man,
he travels round in different moods.
He blows and throws like an angry person,
destroying everything in his path.
The sky now looks green, black and brown.
He can hear the horrible noise of people dying and screaming,
but he doesn't care,
he's a tornado.

As he calms down,
panic finishes and the sea nearby stops clashing and roaring.
The trees stop cracking, swaying and falling,
the grass starts to whistle, gently in the breeze,
leaning gently to one side.
He now tiptoes over the land,
he has realised what he did wrong.
The damage, the death, the danger.
He did wrong.
He then whimpered away.

Liam Palmer (10)
Burbage Junior School

THE WIND

The wind is a mad man
raging like a bull,
demolishing fences
as he pulls.

And when at night
he wakes you up,
and gives you a fright
you wrap your covers around yourself.

On a calm day
with a gentle breeze,
he makes the trees lightly sway,
and sings with the bees in their striped dungarees.

He whips up leaves with his fragile fingers
and howls and howls on a winter day.
He rocks dead trees like a baby in a cradle
and blows the rain clouds away.

Max Stephenson (10)
Burbage Junior School

THE WIND

The wind is like a mad man,
ripping furiously at the trees,
whisking up leaves from the flimsy grass.
He carelessly sways the evergreens.

He bites at tender skins of children,
whistling through the bushes,
he hauls the petals off precarious flowers,
and then he quietly hushes.

He creates the shape of a whirlwind,
swirling past calm trees.
He then falls on to his knees
and dies of exhaustion.

Alex Botting (10)
Burbage Junior School

PANDORA

She is a terror film,
She is a soft drink,
She is the pollen in the flower,
She is a tall sunflower,
She is a hot curry,
Midnight is she,
She is an orange poppy,
She is a hard diamond,
She is a sour lemon,
She is a swept out log.

Jodie Watts (9)
Church Langton Primary School

MEDUSA

Evil
Queen of darkness
Stone cold, eyes bloodshot, dying, dead
Haunting

Suzanne Ward (10)
Church Langton Primary School

PANDORA

She is a thunder storm,
a bright yellow.
She is a cold winter,
a hot curry.
She is midnight,
a parasitic weed.
She is a raging lion.
She is Pandora.

Annie Bladon (9)
Church Langton Primary School

MEDUSA

Darkness
Death lurks at night.
Dread feelings within.
Dented finger marks everywhere.
Death lurks

Nicholas Ruggles (9)
Church Langton Primary School

PANDORA

She is a soft chair,
a soothing melody.
She is a horse galloping,
a breath of wind.
She is a spicy vegetable,
a swept out log.

Kayleigh Hibbert (9)
Church Langton Primary School

PANDORA

She is a breath of wind
She is a cry of sadness
She is the colours of autumn
She is a smooth, gold ring
She is a thorny rose
She is the golden grass
She is the blinding sun.

Kieran Soni (9)
Church Langton Primary School

THE BOX

It is a rough sea,
a poisonous flower,
a sour grape,
a horror film,
a wet season,
and a decaying carcass.

Philip Durno (10)
Church Langton Primary School

PANDORA

She is a sweet summer day,
a dark red material,
a flower in the moonlight,
a red deer jumping over a log.
She is peaceful music,
a smooth, silk chair.

Gavin Hudspith (10)
Church Langton Primary School

PANDORA

She is a new book,
she is yellow sunshine,
an orange poppy.
She is a soft milkshake,
she is an old house,
she is a thunder storm.

Matthew Watson (9)
Church Langton Primary School

THE STORM

Violently
Hurling lightning bolts
Furiously he roars with terror
Gradually
Dies in throbbing agony.

Tom Lambert (11)
Church Langton Primary School

DAYS OF THE WEEK

Monday's here, I get out of bed,
Oops-a-daisy! I bump my head!

It's Tuesday, all fun and play,
Threw at my sister a ball of clay.

Wednesday's boring, it's chucking it down,
I decided to dress up as a clown.

Thursday's here, not again!
This day just drives me insane!

It's Friday, the end of the week,
We need a plumber there's a leak.

Finally! Saturday's here,
Nothing really much to fear.

Sunday lunch, yum yum,
But Monday is soon to come . . .

Emily Slatter (10)
Church Langton Primary School

PANDORA

She is a calm piece played on the piano.
She is a warm breeze.
She is spring.
A bouquet of roses.
She is soft silk.
A towering tree.
She is a soft peach.
She is violet.
She is a bright moon.

Cally Holland (10)
Church Langton Primary School

THE DAYS OF THE WEEK

Monday's here, I'm off to school,
What am I doing? What a fool!

Tuesday's here, today's the game,
6-1 to us they were so tame.

Wednesday's here, detention for me,
Hopefully I'll be home for tea.

Thursday's here, spelling test,
Hopefully I'll beat the rest.

Friday's here, it's half past three,
First one to the gate is me!

Saturday's here, I'm off to the park,
I'm going to see my friend Bart.

Sunday's here, my dad got a Merc,
But I have to stay and do my homework.

Nicholas Hollis (11) & Harry Lewis (10)
Church Langton Primary School

MEDUSA

She is stone cold evil,
grey harshness with striking eyes,
she pounces on life.

Alicia Higham (10)
Church Langton Primary School

MY WEEK

Monday is here again,
Time to pick up my fountain pen.

Tuesday a spelling test!
I promised Mum I'd do my best.

Wednesday we're half way through,
Though now I'm feeling rather blue.

Thursday will the week ever end?
Yes the weekend's just round the bend.

Friday we have some art,
It's nearly time for the weekend to start.

Saturday hooray, the weekend's just begun
Let's go out and have plenty of fun.

Sunday, oh the sorrow,
It's back to school tomorrow.

Katie Muggleton (11)
Church Langton Primary School

I'D LIKE TO PAINT

The heat of the summer sun,
The feeling of the wind sweeping
                            through my fingers,
The sweetness of love,
The touch of sadness,
The freedom of animals,
The cool feeling of rain,
            trickling down my cheek,
The speed of a cheetah.

Ayesha Emilie Edwards (11)
Church Langton Primary School

BLACK CAT

Black cat, staring with resplendent eyes,
You land on cushioned feet.
Your incredible pounce,
Aptitude, you are as cunning as a fox.

You are gifted with a talent,
Many more than a few.
And you wear a gown of death,
Trusting nobody, mysterious creature.
You know secrets that never were told,
And high up in the night sky,
You jump with streamlined body.
You are the night,
You are luck,
You are king of mystery.

Emma Ruggles (11)
Church Langton Primary School

ARMADILLO

You are a bowling ball of youth,
fit in a wolf's mouth shall not.
A perfect gardener are you.
You have your own self-defence.
A slow runner are you,
you are a rolling army tank.
You are a knight in shining armour,
rest you shall not.

Craig Freestone (10)
Church Langton Primary School

WHERE LETTERS LIVE AND WHAT THEY DO THERE!

A is ambling in Australia,
B is bouncing in Bulgaria,
C is climbing in Canada,
D is drinking in Denmark,
E is eating in Egypt,
F is fighting in Finland,
G is gazing in Greece,
H is happy in Holland,
I is ill in Iceland,
J is juggling in Japan,
K is kicking in Kenya,
L is laughing in Libya,
M is miserable in Mexico,
N is naughty in Nepal,
O is obliging in Oman,
P is playing in Poland,
Q is quacking in Qatar,
R is rioting in Romania,
S is singing in Spain,
T is tickling in Turkey,
U is useless in USA,
V is violent in Vietnam,
W is watching in Wales,
X is X-raying in Xining,
Y is yachting in Yugoslavia,
Z is zigzagging in Zambia.

Debora Tugwell (11)
Church Langton Primary School

SEASONS

Spring comes along with April showers,
Easter eggs and dainty flowers.

Summer brings the sweltering weather,
Vacations come, but do not last forever.

Autumn brings the bitter breeze,
That steals the fronds from the trees.

Winter freezes autumn's dew,
Treats at Christmas and turkeys too.

Lucie Hartley (11)
Church Langton Primary School

MEDUSA

The side of darkness,
a flame of blistering fire,
queen of the evil world.

Hissing snakes for hair,
slithering evil demon,
the footpath to hell.

A sickly spirit,
odious evil ghost,
devil of the night.

Rochelle Lambert (9)
Church Langton Primary School

I'D LIKE TO PAINT

The sound of autumn leaves
crunching beneath my feet.
Peace between animals and man.
The indescribable sound of crickets
on a hot summer's night.
The delightful happiness of success.
The feeling of being loved.

Hayley Giles (11)
Church Langton Primary School

I'D LIKE TO PAINT

The heat of the rising sun
The sound of the moving wind
The feeling of the sparkling stars
The smell of the rain dripping down.

The sound of the frost setting on the grass
But I'd like to paint the touch of the air.

Nicola Jayne Robinson (10)
Church Langton Primary School

THE SNOWDROP

I poke my head up
as I awaken from a
never-ending slumber,
opening my frosty fingers.

But in late spring
when everyone's picked
my friends,
I slowly close my fingers
and drift off forever.

Sally Weston (10)
Church Langton Primary School

THE PANTHER

You are as swift as a swallow's flight
Your brunette robe flows sombrely in the
                                    ebony night.
Your sleek paws pad placidly along the
                                    forsaken plains.
Your lenient strides adapt into a rapid
                                        sprint;
The chase begins . . .

Louise Smerdon (11)
Church Langton Primary School

THE HORSE

You sail over the land like a
            summer breeze,
Your mane and tail flow like a
            gentle stream,
Your coat is as yellow as a
            night's moon,
You are as beautiful as a
            newborn butterfly
Released from a chrysalis.

Lucy Parkin (11)
Church Langton Primary School

Firework Night

F   is for friendly people,
I   is for I like fireworks,
R   is for rockets,
E   is for Emma, my friend,
W   is for warning: don't go near the fire,
O   is for oranges,
R   is for red flames on the fire,
K   is for Kirsty, my friend.

N   is for night-time when the fireworks go off,
I   is for indigo,
G   is for Georgina, myself,
H   is for hot sparklers,
T   is for tea, what you have at the end.

Georgina Cullen (8)
Fleckney Primary School

Goldfish

Golden fish, golden fish
Shining so bright
In the sunlight.
It's out from sea
Come to me.
It's in the sun
It's in the moon
Its colours shine for everyone to see.

Kimberley Leiser (8)
Fleckney Primary School

IN THE SPRING

Of all the seasons of the year,
The best I think is spring,
When flowers show their pretty heads,
The birds begin to sing.

The farmer, what a busy man,
He's sowing seeds all day,
The sun and rain will help them grow,
Into a field of hay.

The trees are blossoming all the while,
They make a pretty sight,
The lambs are skipping in the fields,
They're playing day and night.

Naomi Clough (9)
Fleckney Primary School

IF

If I were a cat
        I'd sit on the mat,
If I were a parrot
        I'd eat a carrot,
If I were a fish
        I'd dry a dish,
If I were a giraffe
        I'd take a bath,
If I were a deer
        I'd drink some beer.

Joshua Buck (8)
Fleckney Primary School

IF

If I were Jack
I'd play
On a haystack

        If I were Josh
        I'd be
        Very posh

If I were Alyss
I'd live
In a palace

        If I were Kirsty
        I'd be
        Very thirsty

If I were Hamish
I'd be
Very Danish.

Louis Swann (8)
Fleckney Primary School

LIGHTNING

Lightning lightning
is so frightening

My brother said this is exciting
now I'm frightened

So when you're inside
it's a good place to hide.

Hamish Graham (9)
Fleckney Primary School

IF

If I were Hamish
I'd say
I am painish.

If I were Jack
I'd say
I would be packed.

If I were Mark
I'd say
I would take you to the park.

If I were Jade
I'd say
Get me paid.

If I were Sam
I'd say
Kiss a lamb.

Matthew Dakin (8)
Fleckney Primary School

MY BEST FRIEND

My best friend
Has dark brown hair
She always cares for me
Sometimes silly
Her favourite flower is a lily
Her eyes are brown
But she never frowns.

Nichola Ellison (8)
Fleckney Primary School

IF

If I were a cat
I'd say
I would sit on a mat

If I were a dog
I'd say
I would be a police dog

If I were a giraffe
I'd say
Go for a bath

If I were a bear
I'd say
I've got a lot of hair

If I were a duck
I'd say
I would watch a horse buck.

Zoe Townsend (8)
Fleckney Primary School

IF

If I was Louis I'd say can I have some of your chewy.
If I was Ben I'd say can I come in your den.
If I was Bill I'd say have you taken your pill.
If I was Sam I'd say I would love some of your ham.
If I was Ed I'd say you eat a lot of bread.

Sam McKenna (8)
Fleckney Primary School

ONE DARK NIGHT

One night last week, I was fast asleep,
The sound of howling wind woke me up,
The moon shone brightly
I could see shadows coming from my bedside cup
I saw some shadows on my wall
Some big and some small
I could see cats all pitch black,
Witches with tall hats.
Suddenly I heard someone creeping up the stairs
I was too scared to say who's there,
But then thank God up came my mum
Carrying something that looked like a black and green pot
So I snuggled down and went back to sleep
And for the rest of the night I never made a peep.

Kelly McClymont (9)
Fleckney Primary School

SPRINGTIME

S   is for sunflower
P   is for poppy
R   is for rabbit
I   is for ice-cream
N   is for nest
G   is for my best friend Georgina
T   is for teatime
I   is for ice
M is for Mum
E   is for egg.

Emma Faulkner (8)
Fleckney Primary School

THE LIVING DEAD

It was a dark and dreary night
They saw me it was a fright
They hissed and howled and all that lot
I saw the baby crying in his cot
Then crash and bang they started to fight
I heard them fighting all through the night
When I woke up I felt insane
Then on the floor I saw my brain
When I saw it I tried to stay cool and calm
And on the bed I saw my arm
They started climbing up the wall
I tried acting calm and cool
They started climbing over my bed
Now I see they're practically dead
They started walking round the place
They started ripping up my face
Instead of hands they looked like cats' paws
And on the end the had razor sharp claws
I saw the leader I didn't feel very well
And then he blew me to the bottom of hell.

Joe Riley (9)
Fleckney Primary School

HORSES

Horses galloping free,
How wonderful they can be.
Lots of different colours
Chestnut, bay and dun,
They're lots of fun!

Rachael Handley (9)
Fleckney Primary School

BATTLE

One dark and spooky night,
In the British trenches in World War Two,
British soldiers shot their rifles.
Machine gun posts scanned the German trenches.
The cry of men was terrible,
When the bullets had impact.
The shells screamed as they were fired,
Men shivered with fear.
Shots going in all directions,
Men knew their fate!

Oliver Crompton (9)
Fleckney Primary School

THE RAP MONSTERS

In the deep dark room,
Like the cave of doom,
Were three monsters,
Three monsters
And the monsters said like the sleeping dead,
'I'm gonna get ya,
I'm gonna get ya.'
I slid out of bed
And the monsters said *'Got ya!'*

Abby Lockwood-Jones (9)
Fleckney Primary School

I HATE BATHS

'Do I have to take a bath?'
'Yes.'
'But it's all wet in there.'
'But you have to.'
'I don't care!
I won't take a bath
I would rather die
I would even rather jump out of the sky.
The bath's too cold
The bath's too hot
I'll never go in it,
I'd rather be shot.'

Mark Redfearn (9)
Fleckney Primary School

FIREWORKS

Catherine wheels shoot out light,
Bangers banging in the night,
Jumping jacks in the air,
Sparklers sparkling here and there,
Rockets zooming in the sky,
Helicopters fly very high,
Roman candles spit out flares,
Rush up to the top of the stairs,
To look at fireworks.

Daniel Gluyas (9)
Fleckney Primary School

SOMETHING BLACK

Something black,
Can you guess what it is?
Creeping in the holly,
Can you guess what it is?
Candyfloss coat,
Black as liquorice,
Shines in the moonlight,
Like a silver dream.
Can you guess what it is,
I'll tell you what it is,
It's a black fox
With her cubs,
That's what it is!

Hannah Crabtree (9)
Fleckney Primary School

BATH TIME

Bath time I love
At bath time I jump in the tub
The bath has got bubbles
Hair nice and clean
Toes nice and scenty
I love the bath
My hands nice and shiny
Easy to get in
But not to get out.

Eleanor Moss (9)
Fleckney Primary School

MAGIC LIGHTS

Catherine wheels spinning in the darkness of the night,
Spinning faster than the speed of light.
All the fireworks go *bang bang bang!*
Sausages sizzling in a pan.
Marshmallows burning over the fire,
Rockets exploding higher and higher.
Little kittens miaowing down in the cellar,
Kittens are frightened down in the cellar.
The fireworks have finished,
The kittens are saved from the frightening hour.

Daniela Westwood (9)
Fleckney Primary School

ENCHANTMENT

Birds start singing at the break of dawn,
Horses prance through a silver storm,
Figures dancing gracefully
While the owl sleeps peacefully
Moonlight shines as bright as the sun
Servants yawn when the work is done
Dragons and slayers go together
Enchanted fairy tales forever!

Jessica McCluskey (9)
Fleckney Primary School

DOGS AND CATS

Dogs are so great
Dogs are so cool
Dogs can even swim in
A swimming pool

Cats are even greater
Cats are so fluffy
Cats play with mouse toys
Cats make a funny noise.

Katie Freestone (9)
Fleckney Primary School

STORM

Storm strides about in the sky,
With her wavy black dress.
Lightning flashing from her fingers
And making an awful mess!

Giggling and laughing all night long,
As she makes the houses crumble,
With her long yellow tongue,
Causing people to grumble.

Driving the trees to bend over with force
And making the rubbish fly,
Suddenly a fuse blows - oh no
And then she shouts goodbye!

Caitlin Field (8)
Folville Junior School

THE GIANT'S ANGER

The giant moans and throws his voice,
But it bounces back towards him,
So back again he throws his moan,
Far towards the distant groan.

But the giant, his anger still at high,
Throws a light bulb into a dark sky.
It shatters into a thousand bits
And across the sky the night, it splits.

His anger calms when day comes near,
The damage will soon be done and repaired.
It is gone, that terrible old dead fear,
All the people come out because they cared.

So off he goes to sleep all day,
Sleeps until he's too cross to lay.
Then back he comes all over again,
To give everything more terrible pain.

Lorna Newman Turner (10)
Folville Junior School

A HAUNTING SPELL

Haunting through the town
Birds trembling in their nests
A ghostly spirit creeping cold and white;

Sneaking through gaps in walls,
Giving out an ice cold chill
A screeching noise is following him.

Floating in mid-air.

Quivering leaves, fall off the trees;
Lifted lids off dustbins
He's giving the baby a terrible chill
Suddenly everything's calm and still.

Bethany Townsend (8)
Folville Junior School

SEASONS GAME

The children on the summer beach,
Then lion stretches to his feet,
First sign of him when he shakes his mane,
And the rustling wind roars again and again.

His head turns from side to side,
Out fall hairs as he walks with pride,
He chases away the summer sun
And all the creatures into hibernation.

Golden, orange, brown and red,
The leaves create the animals' beds,
While lion makes us work less hours,
He gives us time to plant new flowers.

Ginger sky in the morning,
Lion roars to give us warning,
He cries until he's knocked down dead,
Then polar bear steals the mane from his head.

Diamond white and crystal frost,
Under the snow, lion is lost,
To eagle, lion did the same,
Spring, summer, autumn and winter play that game.

Eleanor Wintram (10)
Folville Junior School

STARS

They look down at you at night,
with their magical light,
and sometimes make your wishes come true.

They have invisible wings,
and a high voice that sings.
You can't hear their sound,
telling you to dance around.

But when morning appears,
they all disappear
and come back the next dark night,
with their sparkling light.

Leanne Ayres (10)
Folville Junior School

THE WIND

The wild hound shakes itself madly,
He pushes the trees and rattles the leaves
He scampers around shaking himself,
Blowing umbrellas inside out
And blows hats off heads,
Splashing puddles as he gallops down the street
Banging on windows as he passes by.
Soon he runs away
As fast as a greyhound
And everything
Is as calm
As a sleeping dog.

Paul Wormleighton (9)
Folville Junior School

MY DIARY
APRIL 11-12 1941

I cannot sleep but I am tired.
I know they will come soon
Yes -
Far off I hear the engines.
Air-raid sirens should be going off,
Any minute . . .
Now!
Shrill sounds fill the air,
Babies cry all around,
My brothers and sisters, aunties, uncles, cousins,
My mother, my grandmother,
All are awake,
'Come to the underground quickly!'
Mother commands.
A long, long line of scared people make their way down,
Down, the staircase of our home
Through the book-stacked rooms
Smelling musty, dusty, old.
Then the first bombs drop.

In the underground the smells are homely,
Hot drinks in flasks and biscuits
I will wait, wait patiently for what the morning will bring.

1941, April 12,
A once cherished building
Wrecked!
A library with beautiful books
Gone!
And a small building I called home . . .
Demolished!
But - I still have my family!

Millie Lavelle-Martin (11)
Folville Junior School

THE WAR

We can remember the war
Machines bombing, shooting, killing
We can remember, we can remember
The stench of the blood-chilled trenches.
We can remember, we can remember
Germans screaming, British shrieking
The bangs and flashes of bombs that were dropped.
We can remember, we can remember
The cramped space of the Anderson shelter
We can remember
The German surrender and Japanese tragedy
And we can remember the peace.

David Gilbert (11)
Folville Junior School

STORMS

Wild, warring waves
Smashing against hollow caves
Huge cliffs crumbling into the sea
Deafening, dangerous thunder in the sky
As the waves become dangerously high
Destroying the sea creatures' homes
Water washes over the sand
A light warning ships:
This is land!
The light that destroys the darkness.

Sarah Berry (11)
Folville Junior School

THE SPIRIT IN THE WIND

The spirit in the wind ran past me like a fall of leaves,
Sudden and unknown was the spirit in the wind,
Cold and breathless was the spirit in the wind,
The spirit in the wind was a girl of the heavens above,
She danced till the wind's breeze ended.

She was white as the snow,
She wore white emeralds and glowed,
Each time you touch the wind it happens in a sudden flash,
She becomes an illusion in just one touch,
The spirit in the wind was a girl of the heavens above,
She danced till the wind's breeze ended.

Rebecca Grant (8)
Grove Primary School

WATER

Swimming through the water,
Clear, refreshing water,
Looking at the seaweed below.

Swimming through the water,
Watching the crabs scuttle by below:
Colours floating by, fishes swimming along.

Swimming through the water,
Calm, peaceful water where nothing ever happens,
But then coming out into the real world.

Joe Yexley (9)
Hose CE Primary School

THE TIGER

Tiger! Tiger! Stalker of night,
Stalking prey each gloomy night.
Creeping, jumping, jigging around,
Killing prey every night.

Full moon, tiger, stalker of night,
A red deer comes into view,
Creeping up, deer runs, the tiger's off.
Leap, leap, the tiger jumps.

The deer's down on the grass,
The tiger pounds.
Rips the deer open with his sharp teeth.

Tiger! Tiger! Stalker of the night.

Mark Palmer (9)
Hose CE Primary School

THE CHUBBY HEDGEHOGS

Midnight strikes, hedgehogs awake,
Children sleeping, hedgehogs baking,

People snoring, hedgehogs roaring,
Children dreaming, hedgehogs screaming,

Children stirring, hedgehogs purring,
Children are up and hedgehogs are dozing . . . *zzz.*

Imogen Wendler (9)
Hose CE Primary School

MISS SARAH JANE

Miss Sarah Jane,
That little pain
Has teeth made out of pearl
And when it's time, her lesson time
Her head is in a whirl!

Miss Sarah Jane,
That little pain
Lives down on Walker Street
And when it's time, her dinnertime
She dines on stone cold meat!

Miss Sarah Jane,
That little pain
Has hair made of gold thread
And when it's time, her reading time
She says, 'I'm for my bed!'

Miss Sarah Jane,
That little pain
Has a grand midnight feast
And when it's time, her feasting time
She stuffs herself with yeast!

Miss Sarah Jane,
That little pain
Knows that day is dawning
And when it's time, her wake-up time
Then she wakes up yawning!

Miss Sarah Jane,
That little pain
Loves paddling in lakes
And when it's time, her breakfast time
She eats her frosted flakes.

Emily Grocock (10)
Hose CE Primary School

THE HEAVEN TREE

The heaven tree
stands all alone,
in the clouds of
heaven.

The heaven tree
is a famous landmark.
Everyone goes there.

The heaven tree is solid gold,
but that's only what I'm told.

The heaven tree isn't very big,
it's about as big as me.

The heaven tree
doesn't have any leaves,
it's totally bare!

The heaven tree
waits for everyone,
its patience has no end,
I think I'd like it as my friend.

Harriet Louise Day (9)
Hose CE Primary School

THE WIND

The wind blows and whistles too
It makes things come true.

However you can see
The damage on the trees.

The leaves on the floor die in the night
The night is all quiet
The stars are shining bright.

Rebecca Kesterton (8)
Hose CE Primary School

GATHERING IN DRIFTWOOD

I was walking down the beach one day,
Gathering in driftwood.
Then suddenly I saw a man,
Wearing a big green hood.

> He walked closer and closer to me,
> Then he stumbled in the sea.
> He waded in till he got wet knees,
> Then he gave an almighty sneeze.

He waddled in further,
Then turned around.
Then he flew,
Right on dry ground.

> He jumped up high,
> And landed down,
> On a stone cold rock,
> And now I think he's been fed,
> To a greedy croc.

Polly Durrance (8)
Hose CE Primary School

BALEEN THE WHALE

B aleen the mighty evil whale,
A te small little fish,
L ying on his back going round and round,
E vil eyes watching,
E vil whale comes to Baleen,
N earer and nearer it comes.

T he evil whale drags Baleen under the water,
H its him on the head and he falls to the ground,
E at the evil to bits then Baleen,

W ent to play with his loving friend,
H e plays games like racing,
A nd swish and swash his tail goes,
L iving on a huge stone,
E ating fish once more then time to go to bed.

Matthew Kesterton (10)
Hose CE Primary School

WIND

The wind, the wind is blowing,
the wind is strong.
The wind, the wind is powerful
wind, wind you can't get me
I'm in my home.
Wind, wind look at the leaves
falling off the trees.
Wind, wind look at the trees
falling on the ground.

Lee Craven (8)
Hose CE Primary School

PLAYGROUND

P eople laughing all around,
L aughing and giggling and shaking about,
A ll are very jolly kids,
Y apping all day long,
G oing away and coming back,
R unning forward and running back.
O my gosh they're running back,
U gly kids coming back,
N oises bang and noises clash,
D innertime I'd better go back.

Joseph Cornwall (8)
Hose CE Primary School

THE CAT POEM

There once was a cat
Who started to get fat
Her name was Misty
She had a friend called Whisky
She liked to chase mice
And thought that was nice
I give her a hug
She lies on the rug
She plays with a Ping-Pong ball
When she stretches she looks tall
When the black cat comes
Misty's tail gets thick
She arches her back
And spits.

Charlotte Gordon (10)
Newton Burgoland CP School

FAMOUS SEAMUS

Seamus is really famous,
A big softy.
His tail is wafty.
When you come home,
He grins and smirks
That's how it works.
He growls at strangers
And sniffs out dangers.
When you go out
He looks really sad
And that drives you mad.
So that makes him
Big and bad.
He steals food
From your hand,
Although he is not really famous,
He is still my Seamus.

Ben Reeve (9)
Newton Burgoland CP School

NIGHTMARES

N   ightmares are really strange
I   think they are a kind of dream
G   hastly memories flow like a stream
H   airy fingers clasp my arm.
T   hat was very weird
M   onsters and torture, things like that
A   nd a few zombies and guts.
R   ead this poem and be afraid
E   normous giants come to raid
S   trange creatures crack bones like nuts.

Thomas Gordan Elliott (8)
Newton Burgoland CP School

CHASED BY THE HUNT

The bushy-tailed fox jumps out of his den
Looking around, aware of the danger.
He listens carefully,
Nothing there.
In the meadows he plays happily,
Unaware.
He jumps, he runs and he skips about.
Suddenly, he hears a noise,
A barking noise.
Feeling scared he runs and hides,
Peeping from behind a tree.
He sees the hunt go by
They spot the sly red fox, hiding,
The hounds give chase and the fox runs fast
Over fields.
Barking, yapping go the dogs
Horns blasting
The fox loses its energy
It falls to the ground
Terrified it lies
Then still silence
The poor fox is caught.

Erica Cross (10)
Newton Burgoland CP School

Relaxing Ride!

We come to the fence at a rapid rate,
A dog jumps out from under a gate,
With a buck and a jump we turn around
And off we gallop across the woodland ground.
A swarm of birds flies overhead,
The cows run up to the hedge.
Off we gallop down the track
Rumble, rumble,
A tractor drives out,
We swerve out,
The driver shouts!
Suddenly, we freeze
So still,
What is that thing?
Hairy, dirty, big and dull
Oh no, it's a bull!
We spin around
And with a small nudge
We're homeward bound!
Off we go up the track!
Past the tractor,
Past the cows,
Past the dog at the gate,
Down the enclosure at a galloping rate!

What a relaxing ride that was!

Danielle Clark (10)
Newton Burgoland CP School

WASP IN THE CLASSROOM

There it was
A big fat wasp
Flying around
It seemed to be lost
Swat it!
Kill it!
No let it free
I keep quiet
It seemed to like me.

The girls run
The boys scream
And the teacher tries to swat it,
The Head comes in
And closes the door.
The girls hit it
The boys swipe it
The teacher comes to swat it again
And misses!

It landed on the quiet corner curtain
It landed on the chair.
Tom came to hit it
But it stung him unawares.

While all this was going on
Mary got a cup
She put it over the beastly beast
And quickly scooped it up.
She threw it out the window
It flew up into the air

Free at last.

Emma McManus (11)
Newton Burgoland CP School

MY DOG HARVEY

My dog is called Harvey.
He likes digestive biscuits.
He likes chew bones.
If you say, 'Walkies,'
he gets excited.
He likes to rip the wallpaper
in the living room
but there are no marks at all
on the wall.
He loves to chase leaves
across the road.
He loves teasing the cat
next door.
He jumps in the canal
to chase a duck.
He loves to bark at the door
when someone comes.
He's like a guard dog
keeping us safe.

Emma Buttress (10)
Newton Burgoland CP School

A DOG'S LIFE

There he sleeps on the rug,
As quiet as a mouse.
I think he'd rather be on there,
Instead of his cold dog house.

Every day he has a walk,
Just to stay nice and fit.
The neighbours always welcome him,
With fresh potato frites.

I play in my garden,
He likes to join in.
It's nice to see him happy,
Because it makes me grin.

All the children in the park,
Play with him and sing.
When he gets tired he'll go to bed,
Until the next morning.

Samantha Fell (10)
Newton Burgoland CP School

DAYS OF THE WEEK

Monday morning is so boring because you have to get up
after a long rest.
We never get to do anything good.
Tuesday afternoon it is so close to Monday morning.
I'm always tired when I get up.
It's Wednesday evening such a peaceful time.
Such a bright moon and beautiful stars. Such a beautiful time.
Thursday night I go to sleep and wait for Friday to come.
The curtains close it's so dark. I shut my eyes and go to sleep.
Friday midnight, I'm fast asleep. It's nearly the weekend.
At the weekend it's cool, because there is no school.

Emma Haig (7)
Newton Burgoland CP School

THE PLAYSTATION

I get home from school.
PlayStation's cool.
Run up the stairs,
Kick off my shoes,
Get Metal Gear Solid,
From my game rack.
I put in the disc,
I load up my game
I equip my stinger missiles,
Fire them at Liquid Snake
And Metal Gear Rex,
It's much better than Gex.
I destroy Metal Gear Rex,
I save my game,
I turn it off,
I get 'A Bug's Life' from the rack,
I take the roll of Flik the hero ant,
I battle Hopper,
I complete it.
'Dinner Chris,' my mum shouts,
I turn it off
But I can't wait to come back up!

Christian Moroney (10)
Newton Burgoland CP School

WAR!

In the dirty, dark trenches, full of lice.
Or in the cold bunkers,
The soldiers fight!
Fighting for freedom,
Fighting for peace,
Fighting for themselves.
Bombs explode, machine guns blast, rifles bang.
These are the sounds of war.
Soldiers drop dead everywhere. Bits of body fly.
Tanks grind over barbed wire, soldiers and smashed tanks.
When people ran to help wounded men,
They were destroyed themselves.
Trenches are muddy, bunkers are dark.
People are poisoned by poisonous gas,
Choking and coughing.
Fighter planes swoop in, blasting their machine guns,
Or dropping huge mass-destructive bombs.
War is living Hell.
All around you your mates are smashed to bits.
You treasure what food you have.
Gunboats get torpedoed, as do supply ships.
When you have to go over the top,
Your doom awaits you.
Bombs, rifles, gas awaits you.
Those who survive war,
Are haunted by it for the rest of their lives!

Jasper Heaton (11)
Normanton-On-Soar Primary School

TENNIS

T he tennis court is hard as rock, so the balls will bounce a lot.
E veryone likes tennis, especially Dennis the Menace.
N ever worry about you're not going to win, as it's just the joining in.
N obody actually hates the sport, it's just playing on the hard court.
I like tennis, it's one of my favourite sports and I don't mind playing
on those hard courts.
S ome people are better than me but I don't care, but I have my dad to
play with me.

Rachael Ward (10)
Normanton-On-Soar Primary School

AUTUMN

Rusty leaves fall off the trees
And the cold breeze blows them away.
When you go out of your house
There are no children
And it is as quiet as a mouse.
The flowers are all dying and everyone is sighing.
After school when your parents pick you up
You have to run to your car because it is so cold.

Hayley Wilson (10)
Normanton-On-Soar Primary School

SUMMER

Boys and girls come out to play,
On a bright summer's day.
Laughing, playing in the park,
Until it's bedtime,
When it's dark.

In the summer there's less breeze,
With squirrels dancing in the trees.
The sun is shining all day long
To join the cheerful birds singing their song.

Emma Allard (10)
Normanton-On-Soar Primary School

TEATIME

Boys and girls come out to play
And go on the swings and slides
Play tig and sticky spiders
They go into tea
And have fish fingers
To tickle their insiders.

Amy Waldron (10)
Normanton-On-Soar Primary School

A FULL MOON

As the warm wind turns to cold.
A black sheet covers up the night sky.
The moon appears,
A full moon tonight.
Shooting starts fly across the dark sky.
Take a good look,
For the night . . . is . . . dying . . . away.

Victoria Hellier (10)
Normanton-On-Soar Primary School

THE DEVIL'S WAR

The wind was hellish and the mud was cold
The machine gun effulgent, soldiers bold.
The dead, hanging still on the wire
The noise, deafening and dire.

The guns are cocked, ready to shoot,
Ticks and lice in sock, ripped boot.
Committing death to another country
Still fighting for my 'King and country'.

My friend was shot, twice in the head,
I'm having nightmares, shouting in bed
Spitfires rolling across the sky
Mothers cheering, children singing, oh my.

General Carlly, head blown off at sea
People crying, wanting to flee
You think the cane's bad son?
Nothing's worse than those deeds done.

Jack Constant (11)
Old Mill Primary School

CRYSTAL

I once had a dog called Crystal,
Who had her very own pistol.
She shot me in the head,
I thought I was dead.
But I've Heaven to thank,
The bullets were blank.
So if you see a dog holding a gun,
Take my advice - *and run!*

Christopher French (10)
Old Mill Primary School

TORNADO, THE AFTER EFFECTS

The after effects of a tornado are devastating.
People rummaging for food in their collapsed territory.

It is the sound of crest-fallen children, bellowing out to their parents.
Waiting for a heart-warming answer.

It is when people are searching for their beloved ones
under the wreckage of fallen buildings and houses.

It is families trying to salvage all they can
from what used to be their homes.

It is the hearts of the masses.
Affected, broken and torn apart by this natural disaster.

That's the destruction after a tornado!

Sophie Hayward (11)
Old Mill Primary School

MY HABIT

I've got a habit, right.
It annoys everyone, right.
I suppose it'll annoy you, right.
Anyway, last night, right.
I went up to my room, right,
to watch TV and catch up with the gossip
and my dad, right,
said, 'Stop saying right!' right.
So I said, 'Right, okay, I'll stop.'
. . . But . . . I just couldn't help it, right.
Anyhow, right.
Have you guessed what my habit is?

Jennifer Sullivan (10)
Old Mill Primary School

WHAT IS . . .
AN EARTHQUAKE?

An earthquake is a chainsaw
ripping the land into small segments.

It is a pair of scissors
tearing a map into minute fragments.

It is an almighty demand
tracking over the Earth in mammoth sized boots.

It is the Earth nearly collapsing
when a comet pounds against it.

It is the Earth being intimidated
trembling like a pair of maracas.

That's an earthquake!

Lisa Preston (10)
Old Mill Primary School

WHAT IS WAR . . .?

War is a confrontation to see who wins.
It is a sign of death to everyone
and not knowing when it is going to end.
It is abhorrent to the civilisation and a bad compulsion.
It is where people lose their lives
and the entire world will be destroyed.
It is how we open our hearts to see what we are doing
and then all of this will end before the war wins.

That's war!

Natasha McLean Pender
Old Mill Primary School

THE PEA FIGHT

We're sitting in the kitchen,
my baby brother and me.
We're sitting in the kitchen,
as hungry as can be.

Because he hates his bright green peas.
He picks one up but, whoops, he's sneezed.
The pea comes flying across the room
and it lands on my spoon!

I chucked it back at my baby brother,
which made him call out for my mother.
My mum was in the garden using a hose,
when she came in one hit her nose!

She gave us a lecture, a long one too,
about not throwing peas to me, to you.

We're sitting in the kitchen,
my baby brother and me.
We're sitting in the kitchen,
as hungry as can be.

Jasmine Cockerill (10)
Old Mill Primary School

IF I WAS WAR

If I was war I'd destroy everything in my way.
Then I would launch missiles on every city in the world.
I'd send commandos to take out buildings
And spies to watch the enemy
But is that the way to win?

Edward Winnington (10)
Old Mill Primary School

THERE IS SOMETHING IN MY LANTERN

There is something in my lantern,
I've been watching it all night.
I'll tell you what it's like,
It smells like a musky wood
on the coldest day of the year.
It feels like a deadly thorn
being pierced through your heart.
It looks like the Devil dancing
with his evil smirk.
His eyes staring up at you from his glass container.
There *was* something in my lantern,
till I blew it out.

Rebecca Godden (11)
Old Mill Primary School

INGLISH

I cannot spel very well
I find it dificutl to rite good to
My teecher ses my gramer is bad
and I always get a bad report
I can't help mesing about
I wish I coold rite like my frends.
Perhaps if I try hard and stop tawking
about football I will get it righte.
I will practis my speling and form
my leters corectly.
I will lern how to speek good
and maybe I will get better.

Anna Larkins (11)
Old Mill Primary School

FANK YOU

Me ma says *I'ave* no manners,
But I really do try *'ard.*
I say please and *fank* you,
But she says that aint good enough.
She says that I speak funny,
But I *fink* it's alright,
But I practice real *'ard,* in me bed at night.
Then I go down and tell *'er,*
But she sends me straight back up!
But I still say me pleases and *fank* yous.
I *'ate* it when she says, 'Speak proper!'
Right down me *ear'ole!*
But I still say me pleases and *fank* yous.
Know what I mean?

Fanks for *listnin'* mate.

Ruth Bott (11)
Old Mill Primary School

WHAT IS RAIN . . .?

Rain is light droplets
falling from the clouds.

It is dazzling shapes
falling from the trees.

They are everlasting shapes
very hard to see.

Charlotte Smith (10)
Old Mill Primary School

A DOG SO SILLY

There once was a dog so silly
His name was Arthur Billy
He sat on the floor
And gave me his paw
And now his tail's all frilly.

Nicole Arnold (10)
Old Mill Primary School

FESTER

There once was a man from Leicester,
Who's name was the Great Uncle Fester.
He did a trick
With his great magic stick
And out came a woman called Esther.

Hannah Burton (10)
Old Mill Primary School

OLD MILL PILL

There was a man from Old Mill,
Who had to take a pill.
He swallowed it whole,
Turned into a mole.
Now he's climbing a hill.

Sarah Ward (10)
Old Mill Primary School

SAM JAMES PETER REYNOLDS

Once Sam James Peter Reynolds,
Went to Battersea dog kennels.
He picked up two dogs,
They both looked like hogs.
He paid for them and went,
And he got caught in a tent.
Then one day last year,
They walked down to the pier.
They walked down a track,
And the man broke his back.
He was so terribly drained,
And certainly pained.
He never lived again
And he was buried in the rain.

Sam Reynolds (11)
Old Mill Primary School

MADMAN

I saw a madman last night
I'll tell you what he's like.
His hands are like blazing knives
Which knock cement out of the wall.
His nose is like a wasp's sore sting
Which throbs for the rest of the day.
He carries a precipitous chainsaw
Which would annihilate any human being.
His nails are like snakes' tongues.

Sorry . . .
That's my dad!

Jordan Spencer (11)
Old Mill Primary School

A Dog

I've got a dog! I've got a dog!
What a jubilation.
Got a collie, called it Mog,
Had a celebration.

Gave her loads of Pedigree Chum,
She ate it just like that!
But then to go and shock my mum,
Mog ate her Sunday hat!

And then she had to have a pee
But - no - not on Dad's toe!
And everyone except for me
Said, 'That dog's got to go.'

I disagreed, and in the end,
They let young Mog stay.
But now they're driven round the bend -
Mog's gone and run away!

Sarah McSharry (10)
Old Mill Primary School

Tutankhamun

Tutankhamun was the king,
He reigned for a couple of years.
At the age of eighteen he was killed,
Probably stabbed with spears!

The murderers were never found,
If they were, they'd be stabbed to the ground.
Everyone knows about Tutankhamun,
He probably lived in the town of Khartoum.

Sam Estill (10)
Old Mill Primary School

IF ONLY

I hate computers,
They drive me up the wall.
If only I could pick it up
And throw it down the hall.

My brother is on it all day long,
He is gonna' make me mad.
If only I could pick it up,
It would make me really glad.

Whenever the computer is on,
It always makes me tick.
If only I could pick it up,
Oh, it makes me very sick.

I'm really quite bad now,
I don't think I can keep going.
If only I could pick it up
And go back to my sewing.

Hannah Symington (11)
Old Mill Primary School

WHAT IS WAR . . .?

War is an enormous bomb
being dropped on the world.
It is a desperate fight
for survival of life.
It is where each day is hope
that it will end.

That's . . . war!

Rebecca Tongue (11)
Old Mill Primary School

THE BIG MATCH!

We've won our last five games at home,
We're not so good away.
We've got to get ready for the big cup game
At the very start of May.

We've won that cup twice before,
And I'm sure it could be more.
I want us to lift that great big cup
So it goes right up and up.

I've got my ticket here with me,
And you can leave it be.
I want next year to be the same,
Sorry I can't stay, I'm off to the game.

Ryan Kenyon (10)
Old Mill Primary School

JOSH

I have a dog called Josh
who is very, very posh.
He always has a tie
it makes everybody cry.
He eats at the table
tells everyone a fable.
He doesn't chew on slippers
but he chews on Chicken Dippers.

That's Josh!

Hannah Kedie (11)
Old Mill Primary School

WHAT IS . . . STARVATION?

Starvation is when you're limp and weak and feel like falling
to the floor.
It is when you're hungry and desperate for food to live.
It is when you're deprived and don't get any presents or food.
It is when you're desperate for food to fall from Heaven.
It is when you're desperate for someone to bring food over to grow
in your country.

That's starvation!

Wayne Harris (11)
Old Mill Primary School

THE ALIENS

The aliens
Were Australians,
We found that out today.
They came to our house,
Rang the bell,
And asked if they could stay.

My mum said yes,
But I said no.
My sister ran away.
I pulled their trunks,
Called them punks.
Go back to the Milky Way!

Ashley Voss (10)
Old Mill Primary School

HAMSTER

My hamster was big and very fat
He had a hat and scared the cat.
Then he couldn't fit into the wheel
And scared my thin electric eel.
He gnawed his log
And scared the dog.
Then my hamster went in his house
And scared my poor white, skinny mouse.

My hamster was scared of the dog,
Which had a really big log.
Then he was scared of the cat
Who was dragging a big, dead rat.
Then he was shocked by my eel
Because he ate his fattening meal.
Then my mouse
Got on his house.
My mouse said, 'Boo!'
Then went to the loo.
Then he saw my pup
And blew himself up!

Christopher Hinton (10)
Old Mill Primary School

FLYING FROG

There once was a flying frog,
Who was best friends with a dog.
They went for a run,
Then they got done
Because they ate a hog.

David James Mingay (10)
Old Mill Primary School

THE DARK

I'm just a little girl,
who's scared of the dark.
I always have a light on,
in case the dog barks.

I'm just a little girl,
I hate scary horror films.
I've got to have a light on,
because I can always hear the kiln.

I'm just a little girl,
who's just a little scared.
I need a little light,
in case I'm really scared.

But I'm just really glad to say
my parents really care for me every day.

But do they have to turn the light out.

Click. Oh No! Woof!

Aaarrrggghh!

Nicola Knott (11)
Old Mill Primary School

THE BLITZ

Death is roaming down the streets,
like a lost and puzzled boy.
At night we sleep with worry.
Children desolate in the road
not knowing if they will live or die.

Philip Chambers (11)
Old Mill Primary School

WHAT IS . . . NIGHT?

Night is when the sun sinks into the sea.
It is when darkness takes over the day.
It is when God spills black paint over his world.
It is a black cat walking over a wall.

That's night!

Lucy Mulvany (11)
Old Mill Primary School

WHAT IS . . . SUN?

Sun is a hot coin, just been made and thrown into the sky.
It's a red fiery star in the light blue air.
It's a hot ball of fire on a blue blanket.
It's a gas fireball.

That's sun!

Darren Latkowski (10)
Old Mill Primary School

WHAT IS RAIN . . .?

Rain is a giant
crying over me.

It is a cloud
leaking over my den.

It's a drink,
pouring over me.

That's rain!

Clare Alison Wright (10)
Old Mill Primary School

AS THE LIGHTS GO OUT . . .

As the lights go out and life is dead,
He hopes the headless chicken won't cut off his head.

As the lights go out and life is dead,
To escape the mad lunatic he hides under his bed.

As the lights go out and life is dead,
To hide from the ugly monster he goes behind his ted.

As the lights go out and life is dead,
He tries to crawl on to his bed;
But he's too scared to see the dark night.
So he stay under his bed until it's light.

Oliver Stephenson (10)
Orchard CP School, Castle Donington

HOUSES

Houses are big, houses are small.
Some looked like a bouncy ball.
They are red and they are green,
But they're always brown in-between.

Houses are brick, houses are glass,
Some are even made of brass.
Some are soft and some are hard.
Some look like they're made of lard.

I have a house, you have a house,
Though no one has a mouse.

Millie Maddocks (9)
Orchard CP School, Castle Donington

THE WACKY SIMPSONS

Bart is a rascal,
Lisa is so smart,
Marge is a nagger
But Homer is a bragger.

Every day in Springfield,
There is a different case,
Millhouse and Bart have a soap box race.

Bart's always rude,
Lisa's sometimes crude,
Always at school,
Principal Skinner's not very cool,
But Auto is the best.

Maggie is a cuty,
Their aunties are so stupid,
Flanders is a religious bloke,
But Homer just prefers to smoke.

Springfield is a weird place,
But it's not a total disgrace,
      The Simpsons live 'ere.

David Gerrard (9)
Orchard CP School, Castle Donington

SNAKES

Snakes are slithery, slimy and sneaky,
If you are bitten you'll feel a bit peaky.
They shed their skin
And they become very thin.

Slithering, sliding in the grass,
Watch out, watch out, beware, alas.
Some are poisonous, some are not
But all of them hurt a lot.

Daniel Abbey (9)
Orchard CP School, Castle Donington

BLOOD

Ooze, ooze, ooze,
A really bloody nose.
Just like water
Coming out of a hose.

Oooze, ooze, ooze,
A really bloody foot.
Just like lying
In an African hut.

Ooze, ooze, ooze,
A really bloody wrist.
Just like a snake,
Going, hiss, hiss, hiss.

Ooze, ooze, ooze,
A really bloody nose.
Just like water
Coming out of a hose.

Christopher Marshall (9)
Orchard CP School, Castle Donington

TEN PURPLE PUPPIES

Ten purple puppies went to a pantomime;
Once became an actress and then there were nine.

Nine purple puppies went to a fate;
One found a new mate and then there were eight.

Eight purple puppies all travelling in Devon;
One went on a boat trip and then there were seven.

Seven purple puppies all had some Tixylix;
One had too much and then there were six.

Six purple puppies looking in bee hives;
One wasn't interested and then there were five.

Five purple puppies all found a door;
One walked into it and then there were four.

Four purple puppies all jumped with glee;
One jumped far too high and then there were three.

Three purple puppies all went to the zoo;
One became a zoo keeper and then there were two.

Two purple puppies eating a scone;
One didn't want any then there was one.

One lonely puppy went off to Brazil;
To visit Uncle Bill and then there were nil.

Kelly Rayns (10)
Orchard CP School, Castle Donington

Deep Behind The Dustbin

Deep behind the dustbin,
I met a cat called Tess.
My friend thought he was clean,
But I thought he was a mess.

Deep behind the dustbin,
I met a mouse called Larry.
Then I found another mouse,
Which he was going to marry.

Deep behind the dustbin,
I met a dog called Ed.
My friends thought he was lively
But I thought he was quite dead.

Deep behind the dustbin,
I met a lizard called Taylor.
Then a stone fell on him
And then he became a wailer.

Michael Byrne (9)
Orchard CP School, Castle Donington

Beans

One million beans on my dish,
They make me very hungry.
Like oval suns floating in the sky.
Orange eggs from a frog.
Loads of beads ready to be pierced.
Now they're going down my throat.
Like a waterfall.
Yum, yum, yum
I can't wait for more!

Sarra Elliott (10)
Orchard CP School, Castle Donington

UNDERWATER

Underwater
When you see a sneaky snake,
He creeps up on your back,
A shark comes and gives you a snap.
When you look in the mirror
You see a scratch on your face.
When he's ready again he comes
And gives you a claim.
When you're ready it might be a game,
But when he comes again he's ready
For a fight.
He comes
And gives you a bite.

Craig Saddington (10)
Orchard CP School, Castle Donington

JARS ARE FUNNY THINGS!

Fill it with this! Fill it with that!
But not with maniac Matt.
Is it round, is it square,
Look inside what is there?

Tap it, pat it, shake it, roll it,
What noises does it make?
Does it make a rap or does it make a whack?
Bang it, thump it, it will make a bump!

Jars are funny things.

Anthony Watts (10)
Orchard CP School, Castle Donington

TEN HAPPY CATS

Ten happy cats all looking fine;
One broke his leg then there were nine.

Nine happy cats walking on the gate;
One fell off then there were eight.

Eight happy cats walking up to Devon;
One got lost then there were seven.

Seven happy cats playing dirty tricks;
One got bored then there were six.

Six happy cats learning how to drive;
One crashed the car then there were five.

Five happy cats going out to war;
One got killed then there were four.

Four happy cats going out to sea;
One went out too far then there were three.

Three happy cats going to the zoo;
One got a fright then there were two.

Two happy cats met a cat called Don;
One went off then there was one.

One happy cat taking one pill;
One found it too strong then there were nil.

Megan Palframan (10)
Orchard CP School, Castle Donington

TEN SMALL DAREDEVILS

Ten small daredevils all drinking wine;
One had too much and then there were nine.

Nine small daredevils sitting on a gate;
One fell off and then there were eight.

Eight small daredevils went up to Devon;
One said he'd stay up there and then there were seven;

Seven small daredevils all doing tricks;
One knocked himself out and then there were six.

Six small daredevils all doing dives;
One failed to reappear and then there were five.

Five small daredevils all on a see-saw;
One fell off and then there were four.

Four small daredevils all drinking tea;
One got it all on him and then there were three.

Three small daredevils all at the zoo;
One got bitten and then there were two.

Two small daredevils sitting in the sun;
One got frizzled up and then there was one.

One small daredevils without any fun;
He got bored and then there was none.

Hannah Clifton (10)
Orchard CP School, Castle Donington

TEN CHEEPING CHICKS

Ten cheeping chicks sitting on a line;
One fell off and then there were nine.

Nine cheeping chicks sitting on a gate;
One came down and then there were eight.

Eight cheeping chicks all going to Devon;
One said he couldn't and then there were seven.

Seven cheeping chicks picking up sticks;
One dropped them and then there were six.

Six cheeping chicks arriving at Clive's;
One failed to get there and then there were five.

Five cheeping chicks looking at a door;
One walked into it and then there were four.

Four cheeping chicks saw a big bee;
One got stung and then there were three.

Three cheeping chicks went to the zoo;
One got lost and then there were two.

Two cheeping chicks talking to Don;
One didn't stop and then there was one.

One cheeping chick saw Leon;
It suddenly fainted and then there was none.

Leanne Gale (10)
Orchard CP School, Castle Donington

MILLENNIUM BUG

It's small and it's hairy,
It's vicious and mean;
When it goes near a circuit,
It gets rather keen.

Millennium Bug!
Millennium Bug!
Watch out for that Millennium Bug!

It bites and it gobbles,
Your circuit away;
So it won't work
Another day.

Millennium Bug!
Millennium Bug!
Watch out for that Millennium Bug!

So you call in
A bug blaster;
He squirts on some stuff
Which will work faster.

Millennium Bug!
Millennium Bug!
Bye bye Mr Millennium Bug!

Laura Faley (9)
Orchard CP School, Castle Donington

TEN RACING CHEETAHS

Ten racing cheetahs running to the river Rhine;
One fell in and then there were nine.

Nine racing cheetahs eating off a plate;
One had too much and then there were eight.

Eight racing cheetahs flying to Devon;
One crashed there and then there were seven.

Seven racing cheetahs having a big mix;
One didn't get counted and then there were six.

Six racing cheetahs running to a hive;
One got stung and then there were five.

Five racing cheetahs running to the door
One got trapped in and then there were four.

Four racing cheetahs walking to the sea;
One dived in and then there were three.

Three racing cheetahs running to the zoo;
One got eaten up and then there were two.

Two racing cheetahs holding on to their mum;
One let go and then there was one.

One racing cheetah up on a hill;
He fell down and then there were nil.

Marc Ryan (10)
Orchard CP School, Castle Donington

NIGHT FLIGHT

In a little Norfolk village,
The clock struck midnight;
But the pink footed goose
Was setting off for flight.

Strange noises were made by people,
But she didn't even mind;
Traffic and the rumbling of aircraft,
Geese calling of her kind.

The goose took off from the waves,
She broke into flight;
Her movement woke two other geese up,
At the dead of night.

Hayley Sly (10)
Orchard CP School, Castle Donington

MY BROTHER

My brother, oh dear my brother!
My brother annoys me day and night,
He always has to start a fight.
It's never him that gets told off by Mum or Dad,
That makes me really really sad.

My brother, oh dear my brother!
He's always perfect when Mum's around,
Keeps himself to himself and never makes a sound.
But when we're alone he's a real pain,
I almost feel like flushing him down the drain.

Sarah Stallard (9)
Orchard CP School, Castle Donington

THE BIG HUNTER

I saw
The big hunter
In my garden
Prowling about
Looking about.
I saw
The big hunter
In my garden
Looking about for food.
I let
My cat in
And I see the big hunter
Is in my house!

Rebecca Houghton (9)
Orchard CP School, Castle Donington

DREAMING

The things were all whirling around in my head
The planets were glowing so brightly;
The stars were all whizzing outside of my bed
And the moon was shimmering lightly.
The cats' eyes were shining so bright in the dark,
The sun, the moon, the Earth and the stars,
The puppies were barking so loud in the park,
You could probably hear them on Mars.

Hayley Warren (10)
Orchard CP School, Castle Donington

CLOUDS

Clouds make pictures
in the sky
very high,
they fly,
I wonder why?

Helen MacIver (9)
Orchard CP School, Castle Donington

SPIDERS

What I like about spiders is they are furry.
What I hate about spiders is they start creeping around your house.
What I like about spiders is their glossy, sparkling webs.
What I hate about spiders is their fangs.
What I like about spiders is their eight gormless eyes.
What I hate about spiders is they can be dangerous.

Stephen Oliff (10)
Orchard Primary School, Broughton Astley

WHAT I LIKE/HATE ABOUT SPIDERS

What I like about spiders is their different colours,
What I hate about some spiders is that they are poisonous,
What I like about spiders is their long hairy legs,
What I hate about spiders is when they die,
What I like about spiders is when they tickle you,
What I hate about spiders is when they get flushed down the loo.

Charlotte Joanne Kenney (10)
Orchard Primary School, Broughton Astley

MY FUTURE

What will happen in the future?
Will aliens come from Jupiter?
Will seals eat meals in a cafe?
Will something exciting happen,
Every day?

Will there be trips to the moon?
Will there be an electric spoon?
Will dinosaurs come back alive?
Will bees build a giant beehive?

Will snakes swim in lakes?
Will biscuits break?
Will oranges turn pink?
Will goldfish blink?

Will ladybirds have ninety-nine spots?
Will cows carry pots?
Will pigs be yellow?
Will penguins say hello?

Will eggs turn into beds?
Will dogs have ten legs?
Will I get the blame?
Will everything be the same?

Will I be all spotty?
Will ink pens be blotchy?
Will cats learn to sing?
Will the phone still ring?

What will happen in the future?
I want to know, do you?

Jessie Laura Morris (9)
Orchard Primary School, Broughton Astley

MY FUTURE

Will there be peace in the world?
Will all the roads be curled?
Will people live on the moon?
Will there be no more room?
Will everyone have enough food?
Will everyone be in a bad mood?
Will dinosaurs come back alive?
Will people still deep sea dive?
Will there be lots of clean air?
Will there still be polar bears?
Will there still be sunlight
Or will it just be a very long dark night?

Luke Murgatroyd (8)
Orchard Primary School, Broughton Astley

THE CORKSCREW

Nine nitwits niggling over nothing,
Eight elephants evacuated East London,
Seven seals saw someone selling seashells,
Six sealions swimming in saunas full of sand,
Five frilly fish found forgotten treasure,
Four foxes foraging for food,
Three thriving tigers tear their third victim to threads,
Two tiny tarantulas try to poison their prey,
One octopus obtaining obvious information.

Donald Robertson (10)
Orchard Primary School, Broughton Astley

THE CHARGE OF THE FISH BRIGADE

Half an inch, half an inch,
Half an inch onward,
Into Pike Water
Swam the six hundred.

'Forward the fish brigade!
Ravage their scales!' he said.
'Capture the maggots!' he said.
Onward they thundered.

Bubbles to the right of them,
Bubbles to the left of them,
Bubbles to the front of them,
Fins unnumbered.

Crash! - Through the reedy flanks!
Shattered their scaly ranks!
Capture the maggots! Thanks
To the fish brigade!
Noble six hundred.

Sam Williams (9)
Orchard Primary School, Broughton Astley

WHAT I LIKE AND HATE ABOUT SPIDERS

I like spiders when they scare your sister.
I hate spiders when they crawl up your trouser leg.
I like spiders when they make sparkly webs.
I hate spiders when they eat little flies.
I like spiders when they jump on your cat.
I hate spiders when they crawl really fast.

Roxanne Herbert (10)
Orchard Primary School, Broughton Astley

The Charge Of The Dog Brigade

Half a metre, half a metre,
Half a metre onward,
Into Human Valley
Rode the six hundred.

Forward the dog brigade,
'Stop your moans!' he said,
'Capture the bones' he said,
Onward they thundered.

Voices to the right of them,
Voices to the left of them,
Voices at the front of them,
Sounds unnumbered.

Crash - went the human pranks,
Smashed their little pranks,
Captured their bones!
Thanks to the dog brigade,
Noble six hundred.

Michael Shuter (9)
Orchard Primary School, Broughton Astley

Monday's Child

Monday's child comes from hell.
Tuesday's child has an awful smell.
Wednesday's child is a bit of a lad.
Thursday's child is very bad.
Friday's child won't use his potty.
Saturday's child has a red botty.
But the child that's born on the
Seventh day is very cool who loves a sporting day.

Jack Alcock (11)
Orchard Primary School, Broughton Astley

THE CHARGE OF THE DOG BRIGADE

Half a metre, half a metre,
Half a metre onward,
Into cat valley
Rode the six hundred.

'Forward the Dog Brigade!
Ravage their collars!' he said.
'Capture the yowlers!' he said.
Onward they thundered.

Fangs to the right of them,
Fangs to the left of them,
Fangs to the front of them,
Pounces unnumbered.

Crash! - Through the kitten flanks!
Shattered their catty ranks!
Capture their baskets! Thanks
To the Dog Brigade!
Noble six hundred.

Daniel Littlewood (10)
Orchard Primary School, Broughton Astley

MONDAY'S CHILD

Monday's child is crazy and wild,
Tuesday's child is meek and mild,
Wednesday's child eats lots of food,
Thursday's child's extremely rude,
Friday's child is pretty and funny,
Saturday's child has a nose that's runny,
And the child that's born on the seventh day
Throws wobblies if they don't get their own way.

Kylie Sharman (11)
Orchard Primary School, Broughton Astley

OUR TEACHER

My teacher's really kind
Although she's nearly blind,
She walks around with her walking stick
And all the boys take the mick.

In the playground we help her out
But everybody tends to shout,
All the boys kick the ball
And always make the teacher fall.

In our lessons
The boys take her possessions
We love our teacher lots and lots
And love buying her flower pots.

Hannah Whysall & Cara Smith (11)
Orchard Primary School, Broughton Astley

SPIDERS

What I like about spiders is
That they run quickly.
What I hate about spiders is
They are black and ugly.

What I like about spiders is
Their big eight eyes that look at you.
What I hate about spiders is
They have eight long hairy legs.

What I like about spiders is
The really big ones that scare your mum.
What I hate about spiders is
They creep in your homes without asking.

Robert Pell (10)
Orchard Primary School, Broughton Astley

JACK FROST

Jack Frost
is a person
who nibbles
your
fingers and toes,
climbs up
trees, and sprinkles
them with
white dust.
They are
sparkly as
ever and ever.
I am
fast asleep
while he
makes pictures
on my window.

Cherith Johnston (7)
Overdale Junior School

FEAR

I am a knife drawn into your heart,
stopping your life forever.

I am a guillotine cutting off your head
and putting an end to your life.

I am a demon ripping you apart
and eating you down to the bone.

I am death, killing you slowly,
painfully until you are dead.

Ben Harris (9)
PNEU School

FEAR!

I am black and grey,
I make you tremble in bed at night.
I am shaped round.
I cackle screaming at you to wake up.
I make you lie in bed
Terrified of what I might be.
I scream at you.
I send a ringing through your ears.
You will never meet me.
But I will always haunt you
And I will always be there.
I will *never* leave you alone.
I will carry on tormenting you.
I will laugh scornfully.
I will keep you awake.
Thoughts whirling round and round your head.
I am your demon.
I am your fear.
I am your deepest darkest thoughts.
I will live inside you for eternity.
I am your imagination.

Poppy Rebecca Wilson (11)
PNEU School

RAPUNZEL

Our play was Rapunzel
It wasn't very good.
Tom-John was Prince Charming;
Rapunzel, Mary Wood.
She had fair, long golden hair
It was just the part.

When the play was finally here;
Mary Wood was late.
Then when she arrived,
I felt lots of hate.
For her hair was above her ears
And in her hand she held a wig!

Kate Moyle (10)
PNEU School

I CAN SEE

I can see big looming mountains,
which seem to rise up supreme, compared to the
houses made by the people.
I can see scavenger birds keeping a cold eye
open for a feast,
left by the half-dead hunters coming home.

I can see a mystical village
that seems to be infinite on that cold winter's day.
I can see people skating and running on the slippery ice.

Sadly the angel of the night sweeps over the Earth,
like a thousand blackbirds flying through the sky.
I can see people running inside their houses and
going for a night's rest,
waiting for a new day to be born.

Alistair Bowness (10)
PNEU School

FEAR

I am deep and strong,
Over-powering and rough,
Making you feel tiny, weak and helpless.
I get very angry when someone disturbs me.
When I am tormented I rise up and rush,
I fly foam everywhere.
I tower up and crash down.
I cause huge waves and pouring rain.
I am your worst fear,
I am the raging sea in a fearful storm.

Zillah Anderson (11)
PNEU School

FEAR!

I'm all the colours you can think of
Black, blue, pink and green.
I kill you and tear you
To shreds at first sight.
My drooling takes your mind away from you.
When I bark you know death is around the corner.
My gleaming collar means danger to you.
My howling deafens your ears.
I am your fear!
I am a barking dog!

Jason Billows (10)
PNEU School

A Winter Tale

I was outside in the cold damp snow,
as the wind blew chill,
and circled us like a fox
focusing on prey.

We were walking cold and weary,
as each step seemed to take more and more time,
and we tried to set our eye upon our home village,
that had turned to a bare landscape of ice and snow,
going on to infinity.
It was like a dream come true,
as we approached our house
next to the icy lake upon
which stood a bridge covered in snow.

James Wells (10)
PNEU School

Master Winter

The man of cold returns.
Bearing his icicle crown.
He runs amok.
Great peril comes to earth.
He prances across the frost-bitten ground.
Casting bitter ice and frost.
Rivers halt in his presence.
Trees bow down in his grasp.
As he cackles in the moonlit night
The moon begins to fall
And morning draws near.
So he rides into the darkness
On his stone-cold steed.

Lewis Murray (11)
PNEU School

BLEAK WINTER DAY

It is a bleak winter day.
The hunters come home famished
From the freezing woods.

The people are streaming by
On a frozen lake,
Just a flash of bright colours.

The landscape is cold, harsh and mystical
In the background.

The people warming their hands
Round a huge warm fire,
The fire is crackling, spitting,
Hissing and roaring fiercely.

Fran Pirie (10)
PNEU School

RACISM

To treat people different because of their skin,
Is a greatly hurtful and terrible sin,
Whoever does must be a fool,
To treat people different is really so cruel,

The case of Steven Lawrence was truly awful,
But they got away because it was lawful,
After all we invited them; we begged them to stay,
But now after years we treat them this way,
In the future I hope it is fair,
Do not be racist do care.

Rowan Prady (10)
PNEU School

Sir Guillotine

I fall into a deep dream and
drift into a vortex.

I come out kneeling down to a dark castle,

lightning firing and striking my heart like it
was paper.

Down comes the drawbridge and a creature
comes out on an armoured horse

and looks at me with his eyes,

his evil fiery eyes.

He chains me up and imprisons me in his arms

I felt my life draining from me

When I wake up and start the dream
                                                            again!

James Hilton (10)
PNEU School

Fear

I haunt the streets of death.
I run behind every building darkening the light.
As you walk past you think of the deadly things
That could be prowling down there.
I am your fear.
I am your hatred.
I am a dark alley!

Jack Haines (9)
PNEU School

TIDDLES THE GIGGLES

Poor little Tiddles,
She's always got the giggles,
She laughs all the time,
With something on her mind.

She laughs when she's asleep,
Nobody knows why,
She's always full of chuckles,
I've never seen her cry.

She laughs when she is eating,
She laughs when she's at school,
What can be so funny?
There is no one playing the fool.

She laughs in the sitting room,
She laughs when drinking tea
She giggles when she cleans her teeth,
And laughs when she's with me.

She laughs instead of singing,
When we are in prayers.
She laughs when she is shopping,
And everybody stares.

Poor little Tiddles,
She's always got the giggles,
She laughs all the time,
With something on her mind.

Hester Grace Paton (11)
PNEU School

THE THREE LITTLE PIGS

In a land of plenty, not very far away
Three little pigs were there to stay
They collected bricks and straw and wood
Went to a hill and there they stood

'Right!' said the first pig 'away I go
I'm gonna build my house below'
So away went the pig with his clumps of straw
Finished the house, only two more

Away went the second pig with his little sticks
And built his house right next to the bricks
The third little pig took the bricks away
Found a small patch and built his house next day

But along came a wolf with big, *big* jaws
Saw the little pigs and rubbed his paws
The first little pig began to pray
Before wolfie blew his house away

'Yummy' said the wolf, 'at last
I'll really eat this pig quite fast'
It also happened to the second little pig
He also ate his fancy wig

The wolf jogged along to the great river Fouse
Where the third little pig had his big, brick house
The third little pig disappeared inside
And brought out a shotgun, fully-sized!

Oh no wolfie not today
This time I'll be blowing you away!

Simon Lax & Gyles Wilkins (10)
Ridgeway Primary School

THE THREE LITTLE PIGS

Their mother said
You've got big snouts,
It's about time
I kicked you out.

Piggy number one,
Found a man with straw,
He started his house,
With a bright yellow door.

Piggy number two,
Built a house of sticks,
And piggy number three,
Built a house of bricks.

Sitting all alone,
In his house of straw,
Along came the wolf,
And knocked on the door.

He asked to come in,
But the piggy said 'No,'
He didn't give up,
And started to blow.

He blew and he blew,
And with an ear-splitting *crunch!*
The piggy became
The wolf's tasty lunch.

Watching TV
Without a care,
Along came the wolf,
And gave him a scare.

Rat-a-tat-tat,
On the wooden door,
Still very hungry,
He was looking for more.

He blew and he blew,
Till the house fell down,
He was very happy,
When he gobbled him down.

Piggy number three,
Felt very secure,
He wasn't worried,
When someone knocked on the door.

Once again,
The wolf was there,
The piggy just laughed,
And sat in his chair.

He puffed and he puffed,
but it didn't fall down,
He wasn't very happy,
So started to frown.

The big bad wolf,
Was very dumb,
So he went down the chimney,
And burnt his bum.

James Thomas (9)
Ridgeway Primary School

SNOW

Glistening in the morning sky.
Falling gently to the ground.
Cold as ice
And wet as water.
Round and round it swirls.
White like a diamond.
Soft and crunchy.

Slipping sliding in the snow.
Snowmen still as stone.
Cold hands red faces like fire.
Laughter fills the air.
Snowballs everywhere.

Nathanael John Yousuf (10)
Ridgeway Primary School

NATURAL SPLENDOUR

Natural splendour,
Ruined by man,
Eaten by hunters,
Captured by plan,

Likes company,
Lives in herds,
Does not like bits or curbs,

Natural splendour,
Natural horse,
Can we see our equine's source?

Rebecca Yarrow (9)
Ridgeway Primary School

THE EMPEROR'S NEW CLOTHES

The Emperor loved his clothes,
Everyone said, 'Just look at those.'
One day came two weavers,
But really they were thievers.
They asked for lots of money,
And said their clothes were funny.
The clothes were invisible to anyone who's a fool,
You can even wear one in the swimming pool!
He told the weavers that he would pay,
Right on this very day.

The weavers started work straight away,
And said they'd be ready in two nights and a day.
The Emperor sent a minister to see,
If the clothes were nearly ready.
The minister couldn't see a thing,
He said he could then the dinnerbell made a ping!
The Emperor sent another important man who
Couldn't even see one shoe!
At last the Emperor came himself,
How do you think he felt?

At last the clothes were ready,
And the weavers said the shoes were steady.
The Emperor went in the parade,
All the town was afraid!
Then a child said 'He's got nothing on!'
The Emperor just carried on!

Irene Lomer (10)
Ridgeway Primary School

THE EMPEROR'S NEW CLOTHES

The Emperor loved his clothes very much,
Even if they were Spanish or Dutch.
He always wanted the best clothes,
From the top of his head to the tip of his toes.
One day came some knaves,
That used to live in ancient caves.
They soon demanded money
Sweeter than honey!

Nobody could see it if they were foolish,
If you're wise you'll see it as clear as a fish.
'Start work straight away,'
'Then I'll hand your fair pay.'
That's what the Emperor said to the knaves,
Who used to live in ancient caves.
That night they worked on the loom,
And suddenly the loom went ka-boom!

The very next day of the parade,
Everyone watched from child to maid.
A child said 'He's got nothing on,'
But the Emperor just sucked his lemon bon-bon!
At the end of the day,
He threw his new clothes away.

Holly Fitzpatrick (10)
Ridgeway Primary School

THE ROBOT

I know a robot
his name is Johnny,
He is metallic and red
and he can fly,
He is at the cutting edge
of technology
but I don't know why.

He's got a friend called Benjamin
who built him
long before,
But Johnny was
struck by lightning
and remote he is no more.

He is clever and intelligent,
He wants to know the world,
If he finds a
book you're bound to
hear the words 'Input, input!'

Matthew Tester (8)
Ridgeway Primary School

WIND AND RAIN

Shhh, shhh, goes the wind,
Wip wap, wip wap, drops the rain,
Jump, jump, in the puddles making a splash,
Weee, weee, goes the wind and blows the trees,
Tip up, tip up, splash the rain on the roof,
Splash, splash, on my yellow raincoat,
Whoosh, whoosh, and the wind stops the rain.

Jobe Potter (9)
Ridgeway Primary School

SNOW POEM

Snow falls down through the air
like a little bird
landing on the ground looking around.

Eventually it melts like ice-cream
melting really quickly
melting into water.

Then some more snow comes
flying like a rocket
really really fast.

Splash ice comes covering
the ground like
blue grass everywhere here and there.

The ice melts slowly
melting like a snail.

When it all melts no snow or ice left
I am still cold but not so cold.

Georgina Freer (9)
Ridgeway Primary School

WEATHER

Plip plop goes the rain,
Whoo whoo goes the wind,
I can feel in my fingertips,
And feel it in my toes,
My toes
My toes
My toes
I can feel it in my toes.

Splish splash in the puddles,
Getting really wet,
I think it's really fun,
Really fun
Really fun
Really fun
I think it's really fun.

Anna Simpson (10)
Ridgeway Primary School

WHAT IS IT?

The sea is a hungry hamster,
Gnawing in hunger and rage,
As its teeth nibble at its cage.

Clang clang clang the bars shuddered,
As it nibbles and gnaws,
At the bars of its cage.

He digs in the sawdust,
He's like a walking carpet,
He shakes his wet fur over the cliffs.

He is murky brown,
With a white stripe down its middle,
Then he goes to sleep.

He sleeps like a log,
Softly and calmly,
He wakes up.

Then climbs up the bars and
Starts gnawing again!
So he's like the sea really.

Claire Godlington (9)
Ridgeway Primary School

THE CAT WHO HAD A BIG HAT!

There was a cat
Who had a big hat,
The hat grew every nine years,
The cat got smaller every day.

The cat is faster than a cheetah,
The hat is slower than a slug,
The hat hasn't got any legs,
But it slides along the ground.

The hat was so big
He couldn't fit through the cat flap,
He tries so hard he gets his head stuck,
He tries to pull it out but he couldn't.

Scott Barton (8)
Ridgeway Primary School

WEATHER

Hush, hush went the wind,
That was blowing through my hair,
Plitter platter the rain went falling
On my navy blue coat,

The wind was getting louder, louder
And louder,
Splish splosh as I was splashing
Through the puddles with my navy blue coat.

Jade Harris (9)
Ridgeway Primary School

ONE WACKY WHALE WENT WEST

One wacky whale went west.
Two terrible tortoises travelled
to Texas on a tornado.
Three thoughtless thesauruses
thought of a thief.
Four funny fish had fun fussing
about furniture.
Five funny bones went to a funeral
full of fruit.
Six swans sucked six hundred sweets
and started swelling.
Seven students studied in a swimming pool
and survived surgery.
Eight elderly elephants ate empty eggs.
Nine nervous newts next to a noticeable newspaper.
Ten terrified tarantulas taste tails from terrapins.

Suzy Weightman (9)
St Paul's CE Primary School, Woodhouse Eaves

MILLENNIUM

When you hear computers crashing,
When you hear people partying,
When you hear the music blaring,
When you hear World War three starting,
When you hear the bombs bombing,
You know it's the millennium and
You wish you're not asleep.

Ruth Macleod (10)
St Paul's CE Primary School, Woodhouse Eaves

MILLENNIUM - THE END OF THE WORLD?

Just what will the millennium bring?
A horrible alien squidgy thing?
A new type of unbreakable ring
Or they might make our headmaster king!

Just what will this funny dome hold?
A silver bracelet made of gold?
A flying car made in a mould?
Or maybe our teacher will just get dead old!

What will happen on New Year's Eve?
People partying, will they ever leave?
If they do, how bad a hangover will they have?
Maybe if we're not so lucky, they'll make us take a . . .

Bath!

Matthew Hunter (8)
St Paul's CE Primary School, Woodhouse Eaves

THE MILLENNIUM

When you hear the people singing, you know it's time.
When you hear the church bells ringing you know it's time.
When you hear the fireworks swishing, you know it's time.

When you hear people at the door,
Then you're lying on the floor,
You know the millennium's come!

Eleanor Lynn (11)
St Paul's CE Primary School, Woodhouse Eaves

THE MILLENNIUM

When the clocks strike twelve,
We'll hear the ringing of the bells,
And the computers crashing cells,
Will it be the end of the world
Or maybe World War three?

Everyone partying down the street,
Jumping up and down on their feet,
Some of them falling asleep,
And car horns going beep beep beep,
As the millennium closes in.

Hannah Dickerson (10)
St Paul's CE Primary School, Woodhouse Eaves

MILLENNIUM DAY

The millennium comes every thousand years,
The most exciting day of the year,
Sometimes it will crash!
Sometimes it will mash!
But the year seems to dash by,
Maybe it will be technically mad?
Maybe just mad but it will still be fun
For some reason if the world ends we better run!

David Vyner (11)
St Paul's CE Primary School, Woodhouse Eaves

BY THE SEA

Sitting by the seashore, surrounded
by shells
The warm soft sand, beneath my feet
With the waves crashing, the waves
splashing,
All over the beach
Lying in the sun, looking at the
clouds
Drinking soft drinks above the sand
The crabs are snapping, the birds are
flapping
All around the lighthouse.
The bright coloured fish, swimming in
the sea
Jumping with dolphins, for all to see.

Rebecca Loseby (9)
St Peter & Paul's CE (Aided) School, Syston

PIGS

Pigs are so large and pink
I wonder what they really think
They scratch and dig and oink
about
Oh what would they do without
their snout?
They grin and squelch in the thick
brown mud
My, oh my, that looks so good!

Laura Stevens (10)
St Peter & Paul's CE (Aided) School, Syston

MONSTERS

There is a monster
Who lives down the drain
He eats little children
Down a creepy lane.

At midnight
He creeps in the house
He is looking for something
I know, he's going to eat the mouse!

He leaves the house
So I creep down the stairs
I look around
He's eaten the chocolate bears

His name is Hotep
He's from South China
He could be anywhere
Even in your bin liner.

Danny Bradley (9)
St Peter & Paul's CE (Aided) School, Syston

ME

My name is Laura and I love to dance
I do gymnastics and I always prance
I never practise but I always win
I've got no solos 'cause they're all in the bin.

Laura Robyn Adams (9)
St Peter & Paul's CE (Aided) School, Syston

SEASONS

Jack Frost
Cold bitter wind
Large cold drops of wet rain
And slippy ice in round puddles
Snowflake
Slow wind
Sun rising up
April showers bursting
Sweet-smelling flowers are in bloom
Lambs born
Hot sun
No more wet rain
Playing out on the grass
Shorts, shirts, going on holiday
Heatwave
Wet slush
Piles of red leaves
Here comes the blue wet rain
Wool scarves, hats, gloves, warm big thick coats
Bare trees.

Bethany Mills (10)
St Peter & Paul's CE (Aided) School, Syston

THE BUTTERFLY

A butterfly is very colourful.
Its wings are big and graceful,
They sparkle in the sun.
They remind me of jewels tumbling in a chest.
They will always win the beauty contest.

Michaela Bent (9)
St Peter & Paul's CE (Aided) School, Syston

CASTLE

Castles are rotten places.
Dungeons are horrible things.
The knights wore shining armour.
The King with his sparkling diamonds.

The Bishop with his bow and arrow.
You will find hidden treasure chests.
They had a round table.
They ate like pigs.

There were big towers.
The castle was really big.
There were stables.
There were a lot of trapdoors.

There were loads of knights.
They had lots of different weapons.
The King had people's heads chopped off.
People got hung for committing crimes.

Wayne Coleman (10)
St Peter & Paul's CE (Aided) School, Syston

MY DREAMS

I want to be a footballer
I want to be so rich
I want the crowd to cheer
When I come on the pitch

I want to be a goalkeeper
I'm really good at that,
I play for Birstall CC
They call me 'The Cat'.

James Piskula
St Peter & Paul's CE (Aided) School, Syston

THE STRANGEST START TO MY HOLIDAY EVER!

There were piles of luggage in the car,
When a very large spaceship landed from a star,
An alien came out and said 'Hello'
Then I whispered to my dad 'Hadn't we better go?'

The spaceship was silver, with a golden seam,
It sucked us up with a laser beam.
My dad got out, he was really in a rage,
But the alien got him,
And put him in a cage.

I revved the engine, as hard as I could,
And bounced the alien, off the hood,
I saved my dad,
'Hip, hip, hooray!'
So that makes me the heroine of the day.

Frances Farren (10)
St Peter & Paul's CE (Aided) School, Syston

THE MOUSE

My name is Erin and I live in a house
The other day my mum saw a mouse.
She screamed and she screamed at the top of her voice
Then she didn't have a lot of choice.
So she set out a trap in order to catch it
The trap didn't work so she tried to bash it.
She hit it on the head
She hit it on the bum
And then she went and hit her thumb.

Christina Hastie & Erin Hall (10)
St Peter & Paul's CE (Aided) School, Syston

MOUSE IN THE HOUSE

My name is Peter and I live in a house.
The other day my mum saw a mouse.
It ran through the room and out of the door.
We didn't see much of it anymore.
The next day my mum saw another little mouse
So she bopped it and bashed it
And it ran out of the house
So that little mouse wasn't seen anymore.

Peter Barkley (10)
St Peter & Paul's CE (Aided) School, Syston

THINGS!

Big things, small things, things that glow
in the dark.
All things go woof, woof, and bark.
I saw a thing under the bed, I asked it
What its name was and it said Ted.
I've got a real friend and his name is Ted
And he comes from under the bed.
Ted's got a friend who comes to tea and
His name is Davey.

Sam Pallatt-Taylor (10)
St Peter & Paul's CE (Aided) School, Syston

MY HOUSEHOLD

My name's Hannah Baker
As I lay on my couch
Something pinched my bum
Then I said 'Ouch! Ouch!'
Lyn's my mum
And she's sitting at the table
She broke her thumb
Now it's really not stable.
Roger's my dad
Brown's the colour of his eye
He's really sad
But I don't know why.
We're a household of three
We are the best of friends
We've got a strange family
But our friendship never ends.

Hannah Baker (9)
St Peter & Paul's CE (Aided) School, Syston

RAP

My name is Ryan and I swing on my chair
Mrs Hawkins tells me off and says I'm not fair.
I don't like girls or reading a book
I prefer to throw a left hook.
I really like football and Beckham is the best
He is better than all of the rest.
His girlfriend's a Spice Girl, their baby is a boy
And a doll of his mum is his favourite toy.

Ashley Hings (10)
St Peter & Paul's CE (Aided) School, Syston

THE RYAN RAP

Ryan Biddles is a pain in the bum
But when it comes to football he's a lot of fun
He kicks the ball here, he kicks the ball there
He often plays dirty which isn't quite fair
When he gets home he puts the telly on
And then he sees Michael, Jake and John
He's always good at maths
And he always normally laughs
You'll never see him napping
Because he's always rapping.

Ryan Biddles (9)
St Peter & Paul's CE (Aided) School, Syston

CHRISTMAS

On Christmas Eve I cannot sleep,
I want to go downstairs and take a peep,
At all those presents.
I think about things present and past,
I want Christmas Day forever to last.

On Christmas Day, it's fun and great,
I open my presents, and hold out my plate,
But let's not think about Santa Claus,
Hold your head down for a minute and pause.
Christmas isn't about presents or a special toy,
Let's think about Jesus and how he brought great joy.
He suffered in pain,
And I'm quite sure he would do it again.
He died for us because of his love,
But Jesus is now with his Father above.

Lucas Brooks (10)
Sacred Heart RC Primary School

WINTER

Her hair is as pure white as a dove,
She has icy, ghastly features,
Her eyes are as blue as the sky above,
She is a tall, thin, silent creature.

Her icicle fingers clasp the land,
Her bitter breath creates landscapes of sleet,
She hurls crystal hailstones from her hand,
She has the whole world at her feet.

She deprives the land of sunshine,
The coldness stings like a splinter,
Then, she ascends into the sky,
And people call her 'Winter'.

Lauren Thacker (10)
Sacred Heart RC Primary School

CHRISTMAS

C hristmas is a joyful time,
H aving mince pies and Christmas pudding.
R eaching out for Christmas presents,
I magining Santa Claus filling stockings.
S now falling outside the window.
T insel hung on the festive fir tree,
M um clearing up wrapping paper.
A way in the sky, the star shone bright,
S hining above the stable, where the baby Jesus lay.

Katie Fordham (10)
Sacred Heart RC Primary School

WINTER . . .

Snow is a gentle old man, with his snowflakes, white and crisp.
When he settles on the ground, he makes a white sheet all around.
Children come out and play with snow, so white and crisp.
When they pick up the snow, they run inside to get
gloves to make hands warm again.
It gets late and the children go inside and fall asleep in front of the fire
but in the morning, the snow has disappeared.
The gentle old man, who is the snow,
will have to wait once more.

Emidio Chiavetta (11)
Sacred Heart RC Primary School

CHRISTMAS

C hristmas is a joyful time
H ands are joined in celebration
R eindeers high up in the sky
I cicles hanging from the roof
S tockings are hung up by the fire
T ime for the children to go to bed
M idnight Mass for Mum and Dad
A loud clatter heard from upstairs
S anta is here and Christmas is getting closer.

Gillian Haseldine (10)
Sacred Heart RC Primary School

THE MIGHTY WINTER

Winter is an evil old man
Who sends out blizzards and storms
And covers the Earth with a white blanket of snow,
And shoots down hailstones.

Trees are decorated with the snow.
Lakes and streams are a wonderful sight,
Frozen over by Winter's companion,
Jack Frost, who uses all his might.

But although Winter is powerful and mighty,
There is one thing in his way,
The Sun who is the most powerful of all,
And can banish Winter away.

Anthony Marples (11)
Sacred Heart RC Primary School

WINTER

Winter is a skinny but greedy old man,
An ugly old hag who so easily can
Command the snow, the wind and the hail,
To banish all living things, and make them frail.

Winter stretches out his incredibly thin hands,
With long, icy fingers that curl and demand,
That the whole world should be painted white,
To give grown-ups utterly no delight.

But there is one thing of which he is scared.
Something to which he cannot be compared.
The mighty thing is the sun,
And at the sight of him, Winter is done!

James Lucas (10)
Sacred Heart RC Primary School

WINTER

Winter is a cruel, old man
Turning everything grey and dull
But outside, snow covers the land
And the wind blows fiercely.

Winter controls the snow and rain
He tells them to do their part.
They obey their master
And make the whole world miserable.

Children play out in the snow
Wrapped up in warm clothes.
Their cheeks are bitten by the cold
And their breath is like ice.

Winter may be a cruel, harsh thing
But he isn't the lord of all.
He only commands the world
In December, January and February.

Claire Bayley (11)
Sacred Heart RC Primary School

WINTER

W ind blowing energetically
I   ndoors with the blazing fire
N ights are frosty cold
T   he ponds are frozen over
E   very child on the ice
R   eady for the next day.

Marco Chiavetta (11)
Sacred Heart RC Primary School

WINTER

W inter is a very nippy season,
I t's cold outside and fish are dying.
N o one is outside playing.
T ime is going by and spring is coming.
E veryone has their hats on ready to go outside,
R obins are making their nests, ready for the spring.

Kelly-Ann Hill (11)
Sacred Heart RC Primary School

MY SISTER

My sister is grey.
She is a rainy cold day.
She is a near rumbling thunder.
She is a messy desk.
She is a pair of jeans.
She is a whole lot of words.
She is a frozen bucket of water.

Christopher Wells (11)
Sacred Heart RC Primary School

WINTER

W inter is freezing cold,
I n the snow I play.
N asty winter's winds bite me.
T oys everywhere, children everywhere.
E ach home lovely and warm.
R unning around all the Christmas trees.

David Holland (11)
Sacred Heart RC Primary School

MY FRIEND

My friend is bright yellow.
She is a summer's morning in a shady pool.
She is a sunny person.
She is a swimsuit and a tidy room.
She is a game show
and a cool ice-cream.

Natalie Winterflood (10)
Sacred Heart RC Primary School

WINTER

Winter is a cruel bad man,
He commands his friends
To do his dirty work for him,
He plays on the cold frozen lakes -
He orders Wind to blow the trees
And Snow to cover the ground
But when he's had enough,
He'll be as silent as the night.

Calvin Orton (11)
Sacred Heart RC Primary School

WINTER IS HARSH

W inter is harsh in many ways,
I   t's freezing cold and gives you frostbite,
N   o man or woman can stop him coming to kill
      most plant life and make animals hide away in their homes,
T   ogether hail, snow and frost paint the world white,
E   veryone runs from him, except one thing, the Sun,
R   aving and ranting at Winter the Sun chases him away.

Nicholas Dutton (11)
Sacred Heart RC Primary School

A WINTER'S DAY

Walking through the snow, crunch, crunch, crunch,
With a coat, scarf and hat.
Life is frozen, nothing stirs,
The snow is as white as paper,
All the children laugh and caper,
And on their beds all adults lay,
On a cold winter's day.
All the animals are in hibernation,
And all the land is white throughout the nation.
Snowflakes fall, bold and tall,
There's no room to kick a ball.
The farmer stores stacks of hay,
On a cold winter's day.

Chris Nedza (11)
Sacred Heart RC Primary School

CHRISTMAS

C ome and join the celebration,
H oly Jesus has been born.
R unning in the thick white snow,
I ce covers the ground.
S anta will fill your stocking soon,
T he fire is burning brightly,
M um's cooking Christmas pud,
A nd Dad's decorating the Christmas tree.
S o let's celebrate Christmas Day.

Hayley McSwiney (10)
Sacred Heart RC Primary School

CHRISTMAS DAY

Today is time for having a brilliant time!
Rejoicing the birth of Jesus,
Waiting excitedly to open your presents.
Feeling happy for others.
Playing with your presents.
Running outside to build a snowman.
Sitting cosily having a sing-song.
But now it's time for a good night's sleep
For tomorrow is another big day.

Claire Keating (10)
Sacred Heart RC Primary School

WINTER

Hats, scarves, gloves and coats,
We need to put them on,
Jack Frost has brought winter here,
And the summer sun has gone.

Snow, wind, rain and storms,
Are coming from the sky,
Winter's here once again,
So we'll wave summer goodbye!

Jacqueline McLaughlin (11)
Sacred Heart RC Primary School

ANIMALS

I want a snake from Toronto,
And I'm gonna call it Bronto,
But I've already got a parrot,
And its name is Harriet.

My brother's got a spider and I say
'Ow, it's just bit me.'
Now I'm in hospital,
I'm going home tomorrow.

Here I am, safe and well,
As I was saying before
I went into hospital.
My little sister has a slug,
And its name is Splug.

I got the snake from Toronto,
And I called it Bronto,
And it died the very next day.

Rebecca Gibbens (10)
Shelthorpe Primary School

HOLIDAYS

The sun is high in the sky
The sun is hot

People are swimming away
Crabs are creaking away
Waves are crashing away

People are lying down on the beach.

Rachel McKinlay (11)
Shelthorpe Primary School

MIAMI

I wake up in the morning.
The weather's fresh and bright.
I go to get my clothes on
But it is just a fright.
I have got all my clothes ready.
I am ready to go now.
I'm on the plane and
We are going to go now.
I am in Miami
I have never been before.
This place is really big
But some are really small.
This is all I've got to say
This place is really cool.

Daniel Webb (10)
Shelthorpe Primary School

FLOWERS

I see flowers, red, green, pink,
Orange and yellow.
Sunlight, flowers growing.
Bees humming around.

Bees saying 'Flowers, flowers, lovely flowers.'
Beautiful colours in the world.
Pollen sticking to their backs.
It turns night-time, flowers close.
The bees go home.

Kilie Smith (11)
Shelthorpe Primary School

RAMADAN

Ramadan is a special time for Muslims
All my relatives are coming to greet me,
Many dads go to Mosque to pray
And my family breaks their fasts with dates
Dreams of Eid are coming near.
Allah looks after everyone.
Now we can celebrate Eid with our family.

Fahim Agwan (8)
Shenton Primary School

MAN UTD

M an United are simply the best
A lex Ferguson, the Manager
N o-one can defeat the best!

U nited can defeat the best
T ackling their way through
D riving the goalkeeper mad!

Mohammed Moosa (8)
Shenton Primary School

QUICKLY

Quickly the train zoomed past the people.
Quickly the boy ran out of the shop.
Quickly I came to school.
Quickly I ran out of the house.
Quickly the teacher shouted 'Right!'
Quickly I ate my lunch.

Tasneem Khalifa (9)
Shenton Primary School

BOY WITH A BALL

There once was a boy with a ball
And he was very tall.
He gave a loud shout,
The Headmaster came out
And the boy had to stand by the wall.

James Hill (10)
Sherrier CE Primary School

MAD TEACHER

There was once a very mad teacher
Who was a peculiar creature
She saw a bat
She screamed like a cat
She thought it was going to eat her.

Chantelle Wilkinson (9)
Sherrier CE Primary School

DISCO QUEEN

There once was a Disco Queen
Who was an irresistible scene,
Her name was Hannah
As thin as a spanner,
But she really was a 'has been'.

Nikki Shephard (10)
Sherrier CE Primary School

DADDY'S DONKEY

Daddy's donkey was walking one day,
Surely in the best part of May,
Hocus-pocus,
1, 2, 3,
Daddy ends up in the sea.

Daddy's donkey runs away,
Letting out a great big neigh,
Hocus-pocus,
1, 2, 3,
Daddy's donkey ends up free.

Daddy slowly climbs out of the sea,
Daddy's donkey ends up far from free,
Hocus-pocus,
1, 2, 3,
Everyone goes home for tea.

Luke Czerpak (9)
Sherrier CE Primary School

THE ELEPHANT AND THE MOUSE

Mouse was walking in the jungle
And he thought it was a bungle.
Mouse saw an elephant playing tig,
With his friend Lala Pig.
Mouse asked them if he could play
But they said 'Go away.'
But soon they invited him for a romp
And on his body they did stomp.
All their faces went brightly red
Because the little mouse was dead.

Michelle Warren (9)
Sherrier CE Primary School

TIDDLES THE CAT

Tiddles the cat just loved the sun.
She did not care about anyone.

All day long she lay in the yard
And she thought 'Oh my life is so hard!'
Then one day a dog came to call
Tiddles didn't like that at all.

Up she stood, her tail like a brush,
The dog came towards her in a terrible rush.
Round and round the garden they went
Until they were all but spent.
Now Tiddles sleeps on the roof
Out of the way of that nasty woof.

Craig Chester (10)
Sherrier CE Primary School

THE TURTLE AND THE TOASTER AND THE DOG

There once was a turtle who had some toast
He put it in the toaster and burnt his nose.
He got the burnt toast and put it on the side
The dog licked it off the side and ate it like a fly.
The turtle got some more bread and put it in the toaster
He switched it on, it all went wrong
And the bread ended up like a poster.

Ben Tidley (9)
Sherrier CE Primary School

THERE ONCE WAS A CHILD FROM HELL

There once was a child from hell,
Who decided to jump down a well,
It was full of dirt,
And it really hurt,
So now there's a dreadful smell.

Emma Carr (9)
Sherrier CE Primary School

POOR LITTLE PONY

Poor little pony
Grazing on the grass
Nothing to say
Nothing to do
But sit there and
Eat the grass.

So much for that
Little pony
Wandering at night
With no mum to
Love him
Like all the rest.

Abigail Smith (10)
Swallowdale CP School

COLOURS

What is blue?
A whale is blue sailing through the ocean.
What is green?
Grass is green when flowers open in-between.
What is red?
A devil is red, as fierce as a roaring tiger.
What is white?
Clouds are white floating through the air.
What is black?
Coal is black in a plastic sack.

Thomas Earl (11)
Swallowdale CP School

THE LION

There he crawled in the undergrowth grasslands
He carefully eyed his prey as he got ready to attack
He hesitated, then fast as lightning, he pounced forward and jumped
for his prey.

He missed!
He fumbled back up, but his prey had gone,
It was silent, there was no squawking from the birds.
The snake had stopped slithering.
Every animal in the grassland stared at the King.
The lion had lost!

Philip Miller (11)
Swallowdale CP School

COLOUR POEM

What is red?
Redwall Abbey is red, standing strong,
protecting those inside through all weather.

What is green?
Mossflower country is green, its glistening
treetops swirling and waving in the wind.

What is brown?
Skarlath the new-fledged kestrel is brown,
his wings flapping and his feather whistling
as he flies against the snow.

What is white?
Snow is white blowing against Skarlath
and freezing him against a tree in the cold weather.

What is mahogany?
Sunflash's mace is mahogany, whizzing
through the air, slaying a dozen sea rats a second.

Edward Cady (10)
Swallowdale CP School

MY BROTHER

I'm sitting in the front room,
Watching TV,
When my brother comes in,
Then annoys me.
Then I shout at him,
Then I get the blame,
He just laughs at me,
Then I do the same!

Shalene Aley (10)
Swallowdale CP School

THE LION

Out on the sandy plain,
lives the lion again and again.
The King of the Beasts,
is the name that we give him.
A name that's particular,
a name that's peculiar.
But to his friends,
he's John or James.
So there's no need to stare,
for he's out there,
our mate John,
or James.
Yes, our mate James.

Catherine Spencer (11)
Swallowdale CP School

LION

The lion was on the Savannah plain
Showing off his hairy mane,
Roaring, clawing, howling and prowling.
His cubs were having a play-fight,
Which they did by day and night.
He relied on the lioness to hunt and fight
While he sat on his golden hide.
He had a swishy tail
And his eyes were the colour of sparkling ale!

Joe Rudkin (11)
Swallowdale CP School

WHAT IS PINK?

What is pink? A tutu's pink
dazzling so you blink.
What is red? Of course, jam spread
when you put it on your bread.
What is blue? Don't be blue
she loves you.
What is white? A ghost is white
waiting for a fright.
What is yellow? Sweet comes yellow
lovely it is too.
What is green? My home teams
are green.
What is violet? My ring is violet
sparkling in the twilight.
What is orange? Why, an orange
just an orange!

Ellen Sage (11)
Swallowdale CP School

COLOUR

What is white? A plain paper is white,
with a crispness of a new book.
What is blue? The sea is blue,
as we sail towards the horizon.
What is green? The grass is green,
the wind sails through.
What is red? A rose is red,
as it sways in the wind.

Richard Gray (11)
Swallowdale CP School

EMOTIONS

Silence in the exam room,
Silence in me,
A nervous wreck I am,
So don't distract me.

Nervous emotions in me,
Reckless heart mine is,
Covered by a blanket so,
Silence in me.

Questions, questions that's all it is,
But hard as ever, as ever can be.
Please Sir Examiner,
Please read for me,
I will fail, I will fail, please do it for me.

Amy Whatton (11)
Swallowdale CP School

THE CAT

The cat sits there,
Waiting for the string,
The string moves side to side,
Then, as quick as a flash,
She grabs with elation,
The string that tickles,
Torments and tortures.
Then, off like a rocket,
She dashes to her food.

Hollie Freeman (10)
Swallowdale CP School

WHERE, WHERE IS THAT BEAR?

Where, where is that bear?
Is he here, is he there?
I can't find him anywhere!

Where, where is that bear
The tall, brown, shaggy bear?
Oh look!
I am sure I saw that big, brown bear,
Near the tree trunk,
Oh!
That is the bear!

Sarah Laxton (11)
Swallowdale CP School

CAT

Claws, sharp as knives,
Eyes, bright as lights,
In the misty moonlight.

As he scatters through,
The long, silky grass,
Chasing after feisty little rats.

Once the work is done,
And the morning is just begun,
He settles down and cuddles round,
To the mat in front of the fire.

Stephanie Greenall (10)
Swallowdale CP School

SUGAR IS SWEET, BUT NOT AS SWEET AS LOVE

Oh love,
Like a sweet turtle dove,
It fills me with emotions,
Inside my soul.
Her eyes,
Look so cute under the moonlight skies,
Her hair, so long,
Her lips, so sweet,
It's a treat,
Just to look at her.

Oh love,
People say love is cursed,
But I say it is not,
The feeling inside,
So appealing,
I would give my soul,
Just for one kiss
From her,
My love so pure,
Nobody could cure,
That feeling of love at all!

Aaron Grant (11)
Swallowdale CP School

ANIMAL POEM

As the slithery snake slithers by
It suddenly gave out a loud cry
As it gave out a wail
It saw on its tail
A spider, and the snake gave a sigh.

Anthony Hall (11)
Swallowdale CP School

BORED

I am bored
I feel like I am going to explode.
I am listening to a story
Sitting on the floor.
I want to run away,
I want to disappear.
Fifteen minutes till home time
I can't wait to disappear.

Only five minutes to go
I can't wait.
I want to get home
'Have a nice weekend' the teacher says.
Home time
Yes, two days to play!

Emily Keightley (11)
Swallowdale CP School

THE GOLDEN FIGURE

The golden figure moving in its tank
Swimming, swimming faster and faster
All night long.
In the morning, sleeping
Until he has been fed
Then he swims around, eating lots of food.
He comes up to the top wagging his fins
He starts to hide behind his model of a seal.

Zoe Huckerby (11)
Swallowdale CP School

MY HAMSTER

I once had a hamster,
his name was Hammy,
he was the age of 6 months.
And I tried and tried not to cry,
but why did he have to die?

Kylie Mann (10)
Swallowdale CP School

RED ROGER

Red Roger's ruby ring
Red Roger likes to sing
Red Roger always pings
Red Roger lost his ring
Red Roger drinks rum
Red Roger chews gum
Red Roger always hums
Red Roger's ruby ring.

Thomas Clarke (11)
Swallowdale CP School

BLACK

The blinding, back streets go by,
You can't even hear one single sigh,
A black, bobbing broomstick through the night sky,
Not one car went wailing by,
The worried witch went quietly through the dark night,
She found it easy to stay out of sight.

Leanne Marsden (9)
Swallowdale CP School

THE SLOW SNAIL

In a garden slithers the snail,
At any race this snail would fail.
Creeping past the next door's gate,
Hoping he is not too late.
He creeps past the ants' large nest,
The queen stands out above the rest.
He finally arrives at home,
Which is shaped a lot like a dome.
He munches his cabbage and has a drink,
Then he sits down to have a good think,
About the stuff to do the next day,
Which is not very far away.

Sean Paterson (10)
Swallowdale CP School

THE QUARREL

My best friend and I had a fight,
We both went very bright,
It all started off about a pen,
And now she's not my friend,
She said I couldn't borrow it,
So I said 'I don't care,'
And left eating a pear.
I don't know if she's my friend anymore,
But I hope she still lets me borrow the pen though.

Bethany Fisher (10)
Swallowdale CP School

COLOURS

What is green?
Green is the grass
And the leaves on the trees.
What is brown?
Brown is the soil
And the fences in my garden.
What is blue?
Blue is the sky
On a sunny day.
What is white?
White is the colour of snow.
I like making a snowman.

Robert Hoyles (11)
Swallowdale CP School

COLOURS

What is blue? The sky is blue
The sky is up in the clouds.
What is red? A rose is red
The rose is out of the garden.
What is yellow? The sun is yellow
Coming out of the clouds.
What is black? The rain is black
Coming down fast.
What is green? The grass is green
The grass is on the football field.

Dawn McLean (11)
Swallowdale CP School

What Is White?

What is white? Snow is white,
Glowing in the midnight light.
What is blue? Water is blue,
Always rushing thro'.
What is black? A spider is black,
Always ready to attack.
What is grey? A cat is grey,
Walking around all day.
What is brown? Eyes are brown,
Staring down to the ground.
What is green? Grass is green,
Smelling fresh and clean.
What is red? Roses are red,
Sitting in the garden bed.
What is orange? Well, just an orange,
Just a normal orange.

Kayleigh Brooks (10)
Swallowdale CP School

The Big, Brutal Bear

At Brickney Forest stands the big, brutal bear.
Black and proud as he is very rare.
He rips trees and kills nature
And really he does not care
As he bashes and crashes through Brickney Forest.
But he groans and moans whenever he is hurt
But he does not stand for this as he fights his battles alone.

Jack Tomblin (10)
Swallowdale CP School

ALONE

Here I am all alone,
No one to play with,
No one's home.
I wish I had my sister here,
When I talk about her,
All goes quiet.
I wish I had my sister here,
But I don't know where she is.

I wonder what she looks like?
I wonder if she is mean?
I wonder where she is?
She is sweet sixteen
I know that I have one,
But I don't know where she is.

I know that I have one,
I know that she is real,
I wish my sister was here,
But I don't know where she is.

Kirsty Mitchell (11)
Swallowdale CP School

THE OLD HORSE

In the old farmyard stable,
Where the mice go scampering by,
Sleeps a silvered-back old horse,
He never lies down, he just stands up,
And only stirs at the steps of a mouse.

Karl Durrant (10)
Swallowdale CP School

THE QUARREL

My sister is always falling out with me,
She is horrible,
She is grumpy,
She hits me so hard,
When we finish falling
She tells my mum,
I get told off a lot,
I shout at her for telling Mum,
She shouts back louder than me,
Mum shouts at me, I get told to go to my room.
I wish I did not have a horrible sister.

Laura Chandler (11)
Swallowdale CP School

WHAT IS GREEN?

What is green? A leaf is green,
with branches in between.
What is yellow? Corn is yellow,
lying in the meadow.
What is black? A dog is black,
running on the track.
What is blue? A river is blue,
just like new.
What is red? A strawberry is red,
as plump as someone's head.
What is white? A swan is white,
swimming in the night.

Emma Barrett (11)
Swallowdale CP School

BLUE

Light blue becomes the midday sky,
In which the clouds slowly but surely blow by.
New babies' eyes are a beautiful blue,
Dark blue is the colour of the deep sea too.
The sun makes the top of the sea glisten and gleam,
It does this as well to rapid rivers and streams
Blue is the colour you could just float into,
It can represent happiness and sadness too.
Talented tears are blue with success and happiness,
Blue is the ice that strikes with coldness.
You can use blue for anything really . . .
. . . well, very nearly.

Gemma Handley (11)
Swallowdale CP School

THE BEAR

A bear in the woods,
The woods, so green,
The bear, so hairy,
He's after a fox,
The fox, so fast.

The bear, the bear, tears trees down.
He rips the green plants,
He rips, he rips and he rips.

Thomas Luke Freckingham (10)
Swallowdale CP School

WHITE

The white waters freeze
In the cold winter's breeze
In the cool, cold night
When the moon shines so bright
The snow is falling, fluffy and white
So it is ready for when it's light
The white, winter ground
Is spread out all around
Spring is on the way
And soon the white world will fade away
The night sky brightens
And the white world lightens.

Megan Elizabeth Stevens (10)
Swallowdale CP School

MYSELF

I have to learn to live with myself
Every day of my life.
I've got to learn to take all the stress
I've got to take the strife.
Every day when I get home from school
I watch TV, then read.
Then I go on the computer
And do whatever I please.

Carrie-Ann Szopa (11)
Swallowdale CP School

SNITCHED

When my brother and I have a fight,
It's not fair because he always wins.
He never gives me a chance,
So once it's over
He walks away and when he does
I give him a *big* kick.
But then I get sent to my room
Because my brother snitched.

Simon Chalmers (10)
Swallowdale CP School

NIGHT

Dark, gloomy night
a big, black bat
flying with all its might.

Everybody's sleeping
but somewhere in the world
a car alarm is bleeping.

The bat is looking for a bug
but all the children are in bed, snug.

Down by the stream
water chuckles over the rocks
just like a dream.

Now just look above
the sun is arising
so the bat returns to its cave like a dove.

Lesley-Anne Baker (10)
Swannington CE (C) Primary School

FOREST WONDER

When I stroll in the wonderful, frosted forest,
Under my feet the snow turns to flowered snow nests.
The old, oak tree,
All frosted with glee.
The brown, withered cloak,
The old, wise folk.

A shawl of snow covered the ground,
But when I turned around:
The old, oak tree was gleaming bright,
It looks a pleasurable sight,
The brown, withered cloak,
The old, wise folk.

The lovely face loomed,
Out of the gloom.
She spoke not a word,
Not a sound could be heard.
The brown, withered cloak,
The old, wise folk.

Kirsty Anne Bonser (11)
Swannington CE (C) Primary School

NIGHT

Time bomb exploding covering bright blue sky,
Sky, turning sapphire-blue, getting ready for night-time.
Twinkling diamonds, the stars,
One powerful pearl, the moon.
Outlining of thistle bushes creating shadows,
A dove, swiftly swooping over the globe.

Gusty breeze,
Hands clutching stiff, weary bodies.
I stumble on black, greased roads,
I am alone, lost,
I run for home,
I carry on running,
Suddenly I'm home,
And that's all that matters.

Holly Jackson (10)
Swannington CE (C) Primary School

Dark, Gloomy Night

Dark, gloomy night,
Sky, bat-black,
Scared stiff, trembling.

Dark, gloomy night,
Tell myself,
'I'm not scared'
Although I'm shivering.

Dark, gloomy night,
All alone,
Only tall, thin trees,
Moving their wispy branches,
Swaying fingers.

Dark, gloomy night,
Cry out for someone,
Take me back to my warm, cosy cottage,
Sit me by the gleaming, red fire,
Nobody is here.

Chloe Upson (9)
Swannington CE (C) Primary School

SNOW

Snow falling like little girls in sugar-white dresses,
Wrapping the ground with a soft, white blanket.
Icicles hang, witches' frozen fingers,
Shimmering ice, covering ponds.

The moon, cold, glistening in the grey, gloomy sky,
Streams chuckle as I silently walk by.
Fences sparkle in the shine of the silver moon,
The crystal snowflakes wander from the glacial clouds,
Falling softly, slowly.

Rebecca Lawrence (10)
Swannington CE (C) Primary School

SNOW

Snow, steadily, sliding down,
Was a sheet of pure sugar ice,
It lay like an old man's beard,
Soft, gentle.
Soon a beastly blizzard appears,
Hurling down like raining bombs
Exploding on the glacial ground.
Trees, stiff, white witches frozen,
Lakes unblinkable to move,
The creepy, cold moon cries out in sheer terror,
The district, trapped under a layer of silent, white snow.

Gemma Upson (10)
Swannington CE (C) Primary School

DARK

Winter, whistling as it goes,
Drifting ice as it snows.

The cold ice swirls through the sky
The gloomy night-time is nigh.

A little boy runs inside
Where it is his small, safe hide.

The night finally covers all the land
But the snow still falls like sieving sand.

Night won't be there forever
We will beat it, us together.

The snow swirls in a storm,
Like it should, until it is dawn.

Yellow tiger leaping over the land
What a sight, the sunlight, grand.

Gregory Merison (11)
Swannington CE (C) Primary School

SNOW

If snow was a mood, soft and calm it would be,
A blanket of white, filling children's hearts with glee.
If snow was a ghost, ghostly floating it would be,
A house of horrors, scaring you and me.
If snow was a painting, by Van Gogh it would be,
A leaf on the ground from the highest tree.
If snow was food, mashed potato it would be,
Mushy like snow, so I can eat it for tea.

Benn Marsden (10)
Swannington CE (C) Primary School

THE SNOW

It's wonderful when wrapped up warm,
Whilst we're playing on the lawn.
Snow covers the world like a wonderland,
I thought it was beautiful before but now it seems quite bland.
I know how wonderful this all may seem,
But everything has a hidden theme.
Birds can't feed as they usually would,
I try to help but it does no good.
The Abominable Snowman walks through the fields,
We stare at each other but no one yields.
Children think everything's better now the snow is here,
In there, there should be another link it is:
The sky has suddenly become so clear,
The snow has now gone for a year and a day,
The snow is beautiful, it can't go away.

Sarah Jackson (11)
Swannington CE (C) Primary School

WINTER FUN

Winter, whistling as it goes
Children playing as it blows
It is cold on your nose.
Winter, whistling as it goes
Snowflakes falling on your toes
Grandma watching as she sews.
Winter, whistling as it goes
Snowflakes falling on your clothes.

Arron Joyce (11)
Swannington CE (C) Primary School

NIGHT

Dark is falling, like a silky, black sheet,
Wolves are moaning,
The light falls out of sight, bringing on a thousand
fears of a scary night.
As time passes, the hours of darkness gives way to
the power of light, so starts a new day.
The circle is completed, as begins another night,
Another fright.

Jason Ellison (9)
Swannington CE (C) Primary School

I SAW MY GARDEN

I saw a spade glint in the sun
I saw a rose catch the dew
I saw the grass sway in the wind
I saw the creepers bend and rise
I saw a pot crack and rot
I saw a bird eat a worm
I saw the night take its turn
I saw my cat run and sprint
I saw the stars shimmer and glint
I saw the night block out the sun's light.
I saw a spade catch the dew
I saw a rose sway in the wind
I saw the grass bend and rise
I saw the creepers crack and rot
I saw a pot eat a worm
I saw a bird take its turn
I saw the night run and sprint
I saw my cat shimmer and glint
I saw the stars block out the sun's light.

Georgina Elsom (10)
The Latimer CP School

MILLENNIUM POEM

It's five to midnight and I'm waiting,
Holding my breath, anticipating,
I wonder what does the millennium hold?
All the heroes brave and bold,
Three minutes left now, what shall I do?
Have a drink, I need one too!
My mouth is dry,
I have to say 'Bye-bye '99'
Because there's five seconds left,
I'm counting down,
The millennium's here so
Happy New Year!

Shelley Piluke (11)
The Latimer CP School

INVENTIONS

Inventions, inventions, I want to make one too
we might even have robots in the zoo.
There're new ones, old ones
even make you cold ones.
Inventions, inventions, I don't know the truth
if I tried to make one it would go *poof.*
I'll make one, I'll make one, it will go *zoom*
and it might go *Boom! Boom! Boom!*
Inventions, inventions, I won't make one
instead I'll make a large bomb.
        Oh no!

Thomas Chamberlain (10)
The Latimer CP School

THE MILLENNIUM IS FINALLY HERE

The millennium is finally here
Everybody begins to cheer,
Screaming and shouting
Like they're mad.
Celebrating like my dad.
There's a minute to go,
And everyone is silent
Holding their breath
And counting down
5, 4, 3, 2, 1, 0
Happy New Year everyone!

James Ingram (10)
The Latimer CP School

MY BOOKS

When I walk into my library
I think of all the things I've read
Poems, adventures, mysteries, rhymes,
They all fill my head.
My favourite things are books
And everybody looks
When I say,
That my favourite things
Are my very special books.

Katie Williams (10)
The Merton CP School

MY TWO MEMORIES
(Dedicated to Grandad and Auntie Kathy)

I look up to the sky at night
and see a big, bright, shining light.
Who or what is it doing way up there?
I had a little shock and scare.
But then I heard a voice I knew
so quickly it was coming true.
Oh is it, is it what I think?
I could hardly breathe, sneeze or blink.
It's Grandad and Kathy who died two years ago.
I look out for her dress that flows.
She gave me courage and things to play,
and Grandad made us laugh so loud
it made him stand up and be proud.
I love them both so very much
that made me want to pull that clutch
that can pull them down to Earth
and start a whole new big life again.
I'll send this message to you both
I'm tired now, you're fading fast.
We say goodnight, so sleep tight zzzzzzzz

Kaylee Marie Wright (10)
The Merton CP School

WE'RE AFTER THE MILLENNIUM BUG

We're after the Millennium Bug
We're after the Millennium Bug
Creeping round the computer
We're after the Millennium Bug.

We've spotted the Millennium Bug
We've spotted the Millennium Bug
Shoot it quick, we might kill it
We've spotted the Millennium Bug.

We're gaining on the Millennium Bug
We're gaining on the Millennium Bug
Come on guys, we will kill it
We're gaining on the Millennium Bug.

We've killed the Millennium Bug
We've killed the Millennium Bug
There it is, all brightly lit
We've killed the Millennium Bug.

Andrew Smith (10)
The Merton CP School

POLLUTION

Stop stop stop shopping
Pollution, you will destroy the world
This is how you can help
Reduce, reuse and recycle.

Cars and factories will destroy,
The world
You can help by
Not using cars as much.

The animals will die
We won't enjoy good health
Plants will die
The world will be
Destroyed!

Sophie Havelock (9)
Woodland Grange Primary School

CARNIVAL NIGHT

Tonight is the night, it is the carnival.
Come and see the sparkling costumes
coloured gold, red, yellow, green, blue, white, purple and
pink as they dazzle in your eyes.

Hear the steel band play loudly while children
eat sweets, popcorn and candyfloss.
See the brightness of sparklers and floats
covered with spangles.

In-between the floats you will be dazzled
by fire eaters and jugglers and bobbing balloons.
Near the end we see flowers being tossed off the floats.
In the distance you can see the carnival and
you look around and all you can see is space.
The carnival has been!

Sarah Mayne (10)
Woodland Grange Primary School

SCHOOL

Ring, ring, school has started,
All the children have now parted.
All the children cry of bore,
As they enter that school door.
Children gallop,
Children wallop,
Then the teacher shouts out *'Help!'*
All the children start to yelp!

Then at last lunchtime comes,
Lots of food for hungry tums.
Then a little girl called Helen,
Ate a very bitter lemon.
Her face went all red, and puked on a boy called Ted.

That's a day at my crumbling school,
I think I'll buy a power tool.

Rayyan Mughal (10)
Woodland Grange Primary School

SCHOOL LIFE

Oh no, school has started!

One of the pupils is being bad,
Driving the teacher completely mad!
One is writing on the wall,
Another playing with a ball.

And then the teacher bellows, 'That's it,'
'Stop your work, put on your kit.'
Someone says 'It's hockey!'
Another says 'I'd rather be a jockey!'

Hallelujah! School has ended!
Some clever kids are offended,
One says 'Hooray! I can play with my toy!'
Others cry with lots of joy!

Arpan Singla (10)
Woodland Grange Primary School

SPRING MIXED WITH SUMMER

The springtime has come
The flowers have grown
The jewels have come
The blossom has reanimated from last year
The weather is fine, sunny and fun
The summer seasons is bright
And still it is sunny and funny
Days are longer nights are shorter
Still sunny and funny
But now it has come to an end
The blossom is dying leaves are flying
No longer the sun will come.

Sunita Solanki (9)
Woodland Grange Primary School

THE OLD CRONE

The old crone has a face like an old torn carpet
With lips like shrivelled prunes and a red blood colour
She owned orange eyes like burning embers
As bright as the moon at night.

She wore a black cloak
With a hood that covered her hair like old dead plants
Tangled down and down.

The old crone had leathery skin
With long sharp nails
That were stained yellow like a smoker's fingers.

Thomas Hirst (9)
Woodland Grange Primary School

DOGS

I know a dog called Josh,
Who really smelt a lot,
His coat was black and dirty,
He really needs a wash.

I know a dog called Fred,
Who barks an awful lot,
He wakes the neighbours every night,
He never goes to bed.

I know a dog called Mark,
Who never made a sound,
His owner said 'Let's call round Fred,
To teach him how to bark.'

I knew a dog called Shaw,
Who ate an awful lot,
He never stopped, his stomach popped,
And now he is no more.

Late that night,
Josh had a wash,
Fred went to bed,
Mark barked,
And Shaw lived no more.

Akhil Valjee (9)
Woodland Grange Primary School

WHAT WOULD YOU DO?

What would you do
When your mum's mad?
What would you do
When you haven't got a dad?

What would you do
If your brother was greedy?
What would you do
If your sister's eyes went beady?

What would you do
If your uncle is dead?
What would you do
If your auntie is ill and is lying in bed?

What would you do
If your nephew turned to a snail?
What would you do
If your niece turned to a male?

What would you do
If your gran turned to a stone?
What would you do
If your grandad crumbed to bones?

And if I ever turned into a bee
Would my family look after me?

Hanna Ning (9)
Woodland Grange Primary School

THE OLD MAN THAT SMOKED

He puffs all day long,
years ago he did not think anything
was wrong

Time will tell.
He loves the addictive taste, but all
that money, what a waste.

Each cigarette that he takes
death lies in wait
His lungs are worn and his heart is weary,
Is it too late?

Nicotine is in his body,
far in his airways as he gasps for breath.
But he won't give up,
that dirty smelly stuff

His fingers are brown
and his breath smells revolting
Just because of all that smoking.

George Bailey (9)
Woodland Grange Primary School

DRIVING IN MY CAR

Driving in my car
On a wet and windy day

Driving in my car
I've got to get away

Driving in my car
To sunny Saint Tropez

Driving in my car
What a lovely day

Driving in my car
I've got to get away

Driving in my car
To San Diego Bay

Driving in my car
To the pool to play.

Jake Croft (9)
Woodland Grange Primary School